RELIGION AND THE WAR

RELIGION AND THE WAR

BY MEMBERS OF THE FACULTY OF THE SCHOOL OF RELIGION, YALE UNIVERSITY

Edited by

E. HERSHEY SNEATH, PH.D., LL.D.

GYAN

Published by

Gyan Publishing House
5, Ansari Road
Daryaganj, New Delhi-110002
Phone: 011-47034999, 9811692060
E-mail: books@gyanbooks.com

Distribution Network
gyanbooks.com
India, USA, Canada, UK, Australia, France

ISBN : 978-81-212-6434-1 (PB)
First Published, 1918

2nd Impression 2022

Printed at: Gyan Press, Delhi.

RELIGION AND THE WAR
Author: E. HERSHEY SNEATH

RELIGION AND THE WAR

BY MEMBERS OF THE FACULTY OF THE

SCHOOL OF RELIGION, YALE UNIVERSITY

EDITED BY

E. HERSHEY SNEATH, Ph.D., LL.D.

1918

PUBLISHED ON THE FOUNDATION
ESTABLISHED IN MEMORY OF
JAMES WESLEY COOPER
OF THE CLASS OF 1865, YALE COLLEGE

THE present volume is the second work published by the Yale University Press on the James Wesley Cooper Memorial Publication Fund. This Foundation was established March 30, 1918, by a gift to Yale University from Mrs. Ellen H. Cooper in memory of her husband, Rev. James Wesley Cooper, D.D., who was born in New Haven, Connecticut, October 6, 1842, and died in New York City, March 16, 1916. Dr. Cooper was a member of the Class of 1865, Yale College, and for twenty-five years pastor of the South Congregational Church of New Britain, Connecticut. For thirty years he was a corporate member of the American Board of Commissioners for Foreign Missions and from 1885 until the time of his death was a Fellow of Yale University, serving on the Corporation as one of the Successors of the Original Trustees.

Not in dumb resignation,
We lift our hands on high;
Not like the nerveless fatalist,
Content to do and die.
Our faith springs like the eagle's,
That soars to meet the sun,
And cries exulting unto Thee,
"O Lord, Thy will be done."

When tyrant feet are trampling
Upon the common weal,
Thou dost not bid us bend and writhe
Beneath the iron heel;
In Thy name we assert our right
By sword, or tongue, or pen,
And e'en the headsman's axe may flash
Thy message unto men.

Thy will,—it bids the weak be strong;
It bids the strong be just:
No lip to fawn, no hand to beg,
No brow to seek the dust.
Wherever man oppresses man
Beneath the liberal sun,
O Lord, be there, Thine arm made bare,
Thy righteous will be done.

—John Hay.

PREFACE

Religious interests are quite as much involved in the world war as social and political interests. The moral and spiritual issues are tremendous, and the problems that arise concerning "the mighty hopes that make us men,"—hopes that relate to the Kingdom of God on earth,—are such as not only to perplex our most earnest faith, but also to challenge our most consecrated purpose. It is the sincere hope of those who have contributed to this volume that it may prove helpful in the solution of some of these problems.

E. H. S.

Yale University,
August 21, 1918

CONTENTS

I

MORAL AND SPIRITUAL FORCES IN THE WAR

CHARLES REYNOLDS BROWN

In one of our more thoughtful magazines we were favored last February with an article entitled, "Peter Sat by the Fire Warming Himself." It was a bitter, undiscriminating arraignment of the ministers and churches of the United States for their alleged lack of intelligent, sympathetic interest in the war. It was written by an Englishman who for several years has been vacillating between the ministry and secular journalism, but is now the pastor of a small church in northern New York. The vigor of his literary style in trenchant criticism was matched by an equally vigorous disregard for many of the plain facts in the case. His tone, however, was loud and confident, so that the article secured for itself a wide reading.

"What became of the spiritual leaders of America during those thirty-two months when Europe and parts of Asia were passing through Gehenna?" the writer of this article asked in scornful fashion. And then after listing the enormities of the mad military caste which heads up at Potsdam, he asked the clergymen of the United States, "Why were you so scrupulously neutral, so benignly dumb?" His main contention was to the effect that the religious leaders of this country had been altogether negligent of their duty in the present world struggle, and that the churches were small potatoes and few in a hill.

It has been regarded as very good form in certain quarters to cast aspersion upon the ministers of the Gospel. When the war came men began to ask, sometimes with a sneer, and sometimes with a look of pain, "Why did not Christianity prevent the war?" It never seemed to occur to anyone to ask, "Why did not Science prevent the war?". No one supposed that Science would or could. It was the most scientific nation on earth which brought on the war.

It never occurred to anyone to ask, "Why did not Big Business, or the Newspapers, or the Universities prevent the war? No one supposed that commerce or the press or education could avert such disasters. These useful forms of social energy are not strong enough. They do not go deep enough in their hold upon the lives of men to curb those forces of evil which let loose upon the world this frightful war. It was a magnificent tribute which men paid to the might of spiritual forces when they asked, sometimes wistfully, and sometimes scornfully, "Why did not Christianity prevent the war?"

The terrible events of the last four years have taught the world a few lessons which it will not soon forget. They have shown us the utter impotence of certain forces in which some shortsighted people were inclined to put their whole trust: The little toy gods of the Amorites—Evolution, with a capital E, not as the designation of a method which all intelligent people recognize, but as a kind of home-made deity operating on its own behalf! The Zeitgeist, the Spirit of the Age, all in capitals! The "Cosmic Urge," whatever that pretentious phrase may mean in the mouths of those who use it in grandiloquent fashion! The "Stream of Progress," the idea that there are certain resident forces in the physical order itself which make inevitably for human well-being and advance quite apart from any thought of God!

All these have shown themselves no more able to safeguard the welfare of society than so many stone images. They broke down utterly in the presence of those forces of evil which now menace the very fabric of civilization. The forces of self-interest unhallowed and undirected by any finer forms of spiritual energy have covered a whole continent with grief and pain. They have written a most impressive commentary upon that word of the ancient prophet, "The wicked shall be turned into hell, and all the nations that forget God." Men are saying on all sides that unless hope is to be found in religion, in the action of the spirit of the Living God upon the lives of men, then hope there is none. What other guarantee have we that the greed and the lust, the hatred and the ambition of wrong-hearted men may not again wreck the hopes of the race!

But still that question presses for an answer—Why did not these spiritual forces for which Christianity stands prevent the war? I have my own idea about that. It was because we did not have enough of Christianity on hand in those fateful summer days of 1914, and what we had was not always of the right sort. In certain countries the churches had been emphasizing the personal and private virtues of sobriety, chastity, kindliness and the like; they had been preparing the souls of men for residence in a blessed Hereafter. But they had not given adequate attention to the organized life of men in political and economic relations. They had not sufficiently exalted the weightier matters of justice, mercy and truth in the social organism. These things they ought to have done, and not to have left the other undone.

The founder of our faith in the first public address he gave there in the synagogue at Nazareth struck the social note clearly and firmly. "The Spirit of the Lord is upon me because he hath anointed me to preach good tidings to the poor. He hath sent me to bind up the broken-hearted, to preach deliverance to the captives, to set at liberty them that are bruised, and to proclaim"—in all the high places of the organized life of the race—"the acceptable year of the Lord."

This was the platform on which he stood. This indicated the spirit and method of his mission. Organized and corporate righteousness was to be an essential element in the Gospel of the Son of God. The leaders of our Christian faith should have been voicing that same demand for social righteousness all the way from Berlin to Bagdad, and from London to the uttermost parts of the earth. The only Christianity which can avert similar disaster in the future is that Christianity which, like the Apostles of old, goes everywhere, preaching and practising the Gospel of the Kingdom, the sway and rule of the Divine Spirit in all the affairs of men.

It was highly significant, however, that the one nation in Europe which had gone farthest toward an atheistic materialism, toward a philosophy of force, a complete reliance upon physical efficiency and mental cleverness quite apart from any moral considerations, toward a flat indifference to all those manifestations of the religious spirit which are found in public worship, in missionary effort, and in the cultivation of a humble, devout spirit—it was the nation which had gone farthest in that direction which did more than any other nation to bring on the war.

And, conversely, it was that nation which had gone farther than any other nation in Europe toward making the religion of Jesus Christ a power for good in public and in private life which did more than any other single nation in those fateful July days to avert the war, and when war came it was that same nation which did more than any other nation to resist the encroachments of lawlessness and crime as we have seen them in Belgium and in northern France. We have had abundant reason to thank God for the Christianity there was in the lives of such men as Herbert H. Asquith, Arthur J. Balfour, and David Lloyd George, and in the lives of the brave men and women who have nobly sustained them in their righteous contention. We could only have wished that the world had been possessed of a hundred times as much of that sort of Christianity; that would have prevented the war.

And when war came these spiritual forces still had something to say for themselves. Christianity had been pressing home upon the hearts of men those more vital principles until nine-tenths of all the earth was ashamed of the war. Not a single nation was willing to stand up and accept responsibility for bringing it on—not even Germany. That military caste in Potsdam has tried by all manner of intellectual shuffling to save its face by seeking to make it appear to its own people that the war was one of self-defense thrust upon them by unscrupulous enemies. The claim was so absurd that the whole world laughed it to scorn, even before the striking revelations were made by Prince Lichnowsky, the German ambassador at London in the summer of 1914. The effort did, however, serve to make plain the fact that the German Government has not entirely lost the power of being ashamed of itself.

One hundred years ago it was not so. The Napoleonic wars dragged out their weary length for twenty-two sad years, but it never occurred to Napoleon or to France to apologize for those wars which were, for the most part, frankly wars of aggression and conquest. War was taken as a matter of course. It was costly, irrational, inhuman, then as it is now, but it did not have arrayed against it the moral sense of the race as that moral sense has come to be arrayed against this method of settling international difficulties in this twentieth century. In these days war is looked upon by all right-minded nations as the devil's own business, only to be accepted by right-minded nations as a last dire necessity when thrust upon them by governments which scruple not at either honor or right. It is something for the spiritual forces of earth to have accomplished that.

Moreover, when the war came never before in all its history had the world seen so much done in the way of humane service. It has been done to relieve the pain of wounded soldiers and to meet the necessities of those helpless people whose homes have been destroyed by the ravages of war. It has all been done in the name of the Red Cross—the name is significant, as is the spirit behind it. It is the flowering out, not of Buddhism or Mohammedanism, not of some fancy brand of atheism or some philosophy of force—

men do not gather grapes of thorns nor figs from thistles. It is the flowering out of the religion of him who died for men upon a cross.

The people of this country alone came forward and in a single week by voluntary contributions gave one hundred millions of dollars for this humane service. Then within less than a year the same people contributed a further fund of one hundred and seventy millions of dollars for the relief of wounded soldiers and for the relief of stricken people in Belgium and Poland, in Serbia and Armenia, whose names we do not know, whose languages we cannot speak, but whose sufferings we have made our own in warmest sympathy. It was the response of a nation to the words of its Master—"I was hungry and ye fed me. I was naked and ye clothed me. I was sick and in prison and ye visited me. I was a stranger and ye took me in." It is something for the spiritual forces to have thus enthroned the spirit of humane service in the hearts of men.

More than that, never before in military history has so much been done to safeguard the moral welfare of the young men who have been called to the colors. The officers of our own army and of those armies with whom we are allied have by personal example and by public utterance struck a clear, firm note for sobriety and clean living, which cannot be matched in the history of any other war.

The Young Men's Christian Association by its work for the soldiers has leaped at a bound into a place of national and international significance. And the Young Men's Christian Association is simply the Christian church functioning in a particular way. Its honored head, John R. Mott, was converted in and is now a member of the Methodist Episcopal Church. Its secretaries and other workers are drawn, all of them, from the membership of our churches. And the money which makes possible its world-wide activities is given mainly by the people of the churches. The people of this country were asked for thirty-five millions of dollars, and in a single week they oversubscribed the request, giving fifty millions of dollars to carry on this fine form of Christian effort. It was the act of a nation saying to the young men under arms, "Fight your good fight but keep your faith, and finish your course with honor, that there may be laid up for every man of you a crown of rejoicing."

And more than that, the spiritual forces at work in this broad land have kept the motives of our country high and fine. We have not entered into this war with any selfish desire for conquest—as God knows our hearts, we do not covet an acre of territory belonging to any other power on earth. We have not entered this war with any sordid desire for material gain. We were already becoming disgracefully rich in the manufacture of munitions and in furnishing supplies to the belligerent nations. If they could have fought it through without our help, it would have been money in our purse to have stayed out—as it is, it will cost us no one can say how many billions of dollars. We have not entered this war in any spirit of touchiness because our national honor has been offended—it has been offended most grievously, but we are too strong and too sane to plunge a whole country into war for that.

We are not undertaking to punish Germany, greatly as we believe the present government of Germany needs punishing. We remember who it was who said, "Vengeance is mine. I will repay, saith the Lord," and we are content to leave the matter of penalty in his powerful hands. We are not undertaking to dictate to the German people what sort of government they should have. We are willing they should have any sort of government they like, so long as they keep it for home consumption. We believe here that all governments derive their just powers from the consent of the governed. We confess to a frank preference for the methods of democracy, and we could wish no happier lot for any land than to live under the reign of the common people. We like to remember that in the year of our Lord 1815, Great Britain and her Allies put a certain island on the map—they put the island of St. Helena on the map by banishing to that island the disturber of the peace of Europe. And if in the year of our Lord 1919 the United States and her Allies should in similar fashion put some other island on the map by banishing to that island the present disturber of the peace of Europe, nine-tenths of all the human race would rise up and thank God.

We entered upon this war because we were not willing to stand by and allow other nations to be crippled and broken in the resistance they were offering to lawlessness and crime, and in the defense they were making for those principles of justice and freedom which are the glory of our own national history. And so we have come forward to do our part and to fill up that which is lacking in the sacrifices which other nations have been making for the sake of principle.

As I move about among my fellow citizens, north, south, east and west, these are the questions which I find engaging their minds: Is might to be allowed to usurp the place of right, or are we here to see to it that in the long run right is the only might? Is international good faith only an empty phrase, or is it a magnificent reality in the moral world to be upheld at any cost? Is that body of usages and agreements slowly built up by centuries of effort, which constitutes our international law, to be trampled under foot by any nation for the sake of some immediate advantage, or is it meant to be obeyed? Is the whole world to be permanently at the mercy of any military caste which may undertake to impose its will upon the rest of mankind by the practice of frightfulness, or is there possible some such World League of Nations as shall have both the mind and the power to keep the peace and good order of the world?

These are moral questions. They are religious questions, where there is a will of God to be ascertained and realized. And because our people have vision for the full recognition of the place spiritual forces have in the making of history, this struggle enlists the complete moral support of the nation.

It was the moral idealism of the war which brought Great Britain and all her distant colonies promptly into line the moment the moral quality of the German Government stood revealed in all its hideousness by its outrage upon Belgium. It was the moral passion of Britain which enabled her to raise by voluntary enlistment an army of more than five millions of men.

It was the moral idealism of the war which brought all sections of our own country strongly to the support of the President when the fact was made plain that it was a fight for the right of free peoples to live and move and have their being in honor. It was the moral idealism of the war which brought the choicest youth of our land, the sons of good fortune and the sons of toil, the young men of the colleges and the young men less privileged, to stand shoulder to shoulder in this struggle for righteousness. We have seen it on the Campus here at Yale, as other men have seen it in all the colleges and universities of the land. The spirit of our youth has been nobly expressed in those lines on "The Spires of Oxford":

> I saw the spires of Oxford
> As I was passing by,
> The gray spires of Oxford
> Against the pearl-gray sky;
> My heart was with the Oxford men
> Who went abroad to die.
>
> The years go fast in Oxford,
> The golden years and gay.
> The hoary colleges look down
> On careless boys at play;
> But when the bugles sounded war
> They put their games away.

They left the peaceful river,
The cricket field, the quad,
The shaven lawns of Oxford
To seek a bloody sod;
They gave their merry youth away
For country and for God.

God rest you happy, gentlemen,
Who laid your good lives down,
Who took the khaki and the gun
Instead of cap and gown.
God bring you to a fairer place
Than even Oxford town.

It was a great Christian statesman, it was William Ewart Gladstone, prime minister of Great Britain, who said more than thirty years ago, "The greatest triumph of the twentieth century will be the enthronement of the idea of public right as the governing idea in the affairs of Europe." We are here this day to assist with the last ounce of our strength and with the full might of our moral purpose in the enthronement and the coronation of that idea of public right as the governing idea in the affairs of the whole world.

The moral values which are at stake in all this national and international action have been made so clear in the fierce red light which has beat upon the world that the very conscience of the country has put on khaki. The moral sense of the whole nation has become militant. The brave men and women of this land are working and fighting for human betterment with their eyes upon that social order which hath foundations whose builder and maker is God. And because we feel that our cause is just, we feel in our arms and in our hearts, each man of us, the strength of ten.

May we not believe that this country, strong and brave, generous and hopeful, is called of God to be in its own way a Messianic nation in whose mighty unfolding life all the nations of the earth may be blessed? Hear these words of an ancient prophet and make them your own! "What people has God so nigh unto them as the Lord our God is in all things that we call upon Him for? Has God assayed to take him a nation from the midst of another nation by signs, by wonders and by war, as the Lord hath done for you? Did ever a people hear the Voice of God speaking out of the midst of the fire as thou hast heard? What nation has statutes and judgments so righteous as the law which I set before you this day? Keep therefore and do them, for this is your wisdom and your understanding among the nations."

It is for this country to keep its motives high and fine, to set its affections upon those principles of action which are above the dead level of self-interest, and to so bear itself in the service of the higher civilization that in its purposes and methods all the nations of the earth may be blessed.

> O beautiful my country, ours once more,
> What were our lives without thee,
> What all our lives to save thee!
> We reck not what we give thee,
> We will not dare to doubt thee,
> But ask whatever else and we will dare.

II

GOD AND HISTORY

DOUGLAS CLYDE MACINTOSH

Most urgent among the religious problems of the day is the question as to the relation of God to the events of current history. As was to be expected, many erroneous notions are prevalent concerning divine providence and the present war. Some of these errors are owing to intellectual confusion; others, however, impress one as due to an almost wilful perversion of the impulses of religious faith. In any case, most conspicuous among the erroneous doctrines of the day with reference to divine providence is that voiced by the German Emperor, in speaking of the Teutonic triumph over disorganized Russia. His words are reported as follows: "The complete victory fills me with gratitude. It permits us to live again one of those great moments in which we can reverently admire God's hand in history. What turn events have taken is by the disposition of God." One could scarcely be blamed for inferring that the Kaiser imagines, or affects to believe, that the Almighty has entered into a favored-nation treaty of some sort with Germany. But even this would seem to fall short of what is claimed. We quote further from the same theological authority. "The year 1917 with its great battles has proved," he asserts, with almost incredible simple-mindedness, "that the German people has in the Lord of Creation above an unconditional and avowed ally on whom it can absolutely rely." This curious reversion to religious tribalism in the case of the German Emperor is not without its parallel in the belief of his subjects. Assiduously taught, as they have been, that they are fighting a justified defensive war, and praying, as they have been, for victory over their enemies, their conviction has come to be, pretty generally, what a German-American in the early days of the war expressed in these words, "If Germany doesn't win this war, there is no God!" Well, in view of what the world knows as to the causation and the conduct of this war on the part of Germany, the only answer so preposterous a doctrine deserves is that given by ex-President Taft, "Germany has mistaken the devil for God!"

But the Germans are not the only ones who are cherishing mistaken notions as to the providence of God in human affairs. We and our Allies reject the idea of a national God, and any notion of the "Lord of Creation" being our "unconditional ally." The morally perfect God is too just and impartial to have any favorites among the nations, whether Jewish, or German, or British, or American. Might does not make right, we know; and no more is might an infallible index to God's will. God is not necessarily "on the side of the heaviest battalions." On the contrary, the true God, as the God of righteousness, must be, we feel sure, on the side of right and justice, whichever side that may be. Being confident, therefore, of the justice of our cause, we feel that we have the best of reasons for believing that we are fighting on the side of God, as well as for the true well-being of humanity.

So far, good; but many among us proceed to put two and two together and find that they make five. If we are on the side of human rights and the will of God, and if God is sufficient for our religious needs, is it not clear that we may be absolutely certain of winning the war, whatever temporary reverses may have to be encountered? Moreover, especially since we have had our days of prayer for victory, are we not entitled to sing,

> Then conquer we must, for our cause it is just,
> And this be our motto, "In God is our trust"?

Indeed, so satisfied are we with the logic of our position that multitudes of us would agree with the sentiment expressed by a

British-American in the early days of the war, "If Germany wins this war, there is no God."

But there are reasons for doubting the correctness of this view. Right makes God's will, surely enough; but is it certain that the side whose cause is just will win the war, simply because it is the side of right and of God? Ultimately, we may be sure, right must prevail, for wrong is not the sort of thing that can permanently succeed; it contains within itself the germs of its own ultimate destruction. But nothing in history can be surer than that this ultimate judgment upon evil does not necessarily involve the defeat of all unjustified military undertakings. The side with the greater moral justification has not always won its battles, nor even its wars. It is not enough to have justice on our side; we must use our might on the side of right. Right has to be worked for, and sometimes it has to be fought for. That is the kind of world that—not unfortunately for our development, probably—we are living in. And the fighting is no sham battle. Its issue is not predetermined. It is being decided while the fighting is going on.

Moreover, with reference to prayer as a military factor, it is only fair to note that in the present war many sincere and believing prayers for victory have been offered on both sides. It is not intended to deny that religion of a certain sort is an important military factor; sincere and believing prayer for a cause that is regarded as sacred and just undoubtedly helps morale, both in the army and throughout the nation. But it is a factor which in this war has operated on both sides. Man has the capacity for misusing not only physical, but even spiritual forces. But, on the other hand, when prayer and religious faith encourage an easy-going attitude, and are thus made to some extent a substitute for effort, such prayer and faith cannot but prove a serious military hindrance, no matter how just the cause may be that they are designed to support. They may even conceivably make enough of a difference on the wrong side to lead to the defeat of righteousness.

These notions as to God's providence in war, which we have criticized as manifestly mistaken and dangerously misleading, are symptomatic of confused and muddy thinking on the whole subject of the providence of God in human history. How does God secure his adequate providential control of the course of history? One theory is that he has secured it by having absolutely predetermined from the beginning all events of nature and history, so that all process is the simple unfolding of what has been eternally decreed. There are the strongest ethical and religious reasons for refusing to accept this unproved and unprovable dogma. On the one hand, it would mean that man's consciousness of free agency and moral responsibility would have to be regarded as quite illusory, since what has been decided and made inevitable before man's life began cannot have been originated by man himself. On the other hand, this predestination doctrine would mean that God should be regarded as the real and responsible cause of all evil, including what we call human sin. No such God would be moral enough to be trustworthy or deserving of human adoration.

Another theory as to how God secures his adequate providential control of the course of events is that it is by various sorts of arbitrary or unconditioned interventions in external nature, as well as in human life, in order to realize the ends he may desire to accomplish from time to time. It has often been suggested, for instance, that a miracle of this sort took place at the Marne, preventing the German entry into Paris. But this theory is open to the objection that it raises three unanswerable questions. In the first place, how can we be sure that such interventions have taken place, particularly in the external world? How do you suppose it will ever be established sufficiently for confident rational belief, that only by special miracle were the German armies turned back from Paris in 1914? In the second place, if such special miraculous interventions do take place for the sake of preventing evil, why do they not take place oftener, especially in these times of unprecedented disaster to human life? A miracle like that of the Marne, such as would have turned the Turks back from the helpless Armenians, would have been much appreciated. But, for a third question, if such miracles were to take place as often as this theory of providence would seem to call for, what would become of the order of nature, and how could man learn what to expect, or how to adjust himself to his environment?

As against these theories of absolute predetermination and arbitrary intervention, we may point out that God secures his adequate providential control of the course of history in two principal ways, viz., by *enough* predetermination of events to give man a dependable universe to live in and learn from, and by *enough* intervention to admit of a response to man's need of the religious experience of salvation, that is, of being inwardly or spiritually prepared to meet in the right way and with triumphant spirit the very worst that the future may bring. The predetermined order of the laws of nature and mind exhibits the *general providence* of God. By means of this order, or in the light of consequences, God is teaching man both science and morality, that is, how to adapt means to the realization of ends, and what ideals and principles of action must be employed if the most desirable results are to be obtained. The "intervention enough" of which we spoke—if indeed it is to be called intervention—or, in other words, the response of the divine Reality to the right religious attitude on the part of man, is an exhibition of the *special providence* of God. When one has found the right relation to God and gained access to the divine power for the inner life, one is virtually prepared for whatever can happen to him. But, as we have indicated, his preparedness is primarily inner, spiritual. He is in a position to meet danger with moral courage, to gain the victory over temptation; to make the most of opportunities for service; to endure hardship, pain and privation, as a good soldier, with patience and cheerfulness; to face death—his own or that of others—and whatever there may be after death, with faith and equanimity.

There are two possible ways, then, in which God may exercise his providence in the events of human history. There is his shorter and preferred method, and his longer and more roundabout method. If the individuals concerned come into the right relation to God, there is the best possible guarantee that they will be made ready for all there may be for them to do and to experience, and thus conditions will be most favorable for the speedy realization of the will of God. But if this shorter, preferred method cannot be employed, because men fail to rise to the occasion as they might if they would rightly relate themselves to God, the divine providence will still be exercised, although necessarily in the less desirable, more roundabout way. God will let man choose the wrong way, through thoughtlessness or wilfulness, and then let him take the bitter consequences of failure, that he may finally learn to guard against similar mistakes and faults in the future.

Let us now return to the more particular question of the relation of the providence of God to the present war. Before discussing again the question with which we started, viz., as to the final outcome of the conflict, we may deal with some other aspects of the problem. In the light of what has been said of the two possible methods of divine providence, it may be denied that the war was providentially caused by God in order to curb other evils, such as softness and idleness, or the selfish pursuit of wealth and pleasure, or drunkenness and vice, or thoughtlessness and irreligion. It is true enough that in the face of war conditions some of these evils have been decreased, and the martial qualities of self-sacrificing courage and fortitude have been stimulated. But it is notoriously true that the advent of war introduces a host of evils, in some cases necessarily, in others almost as inevitably. Drunkenness tends to increase greatly, unless stern measures are taken for its repression. Vice, with the resulting transmissible diseases, ordinarily becomes much more prevalent. Hatred, cruelty, and even the most fiendish brutality are given ample opportunity to develop, and in many instances they become relatively fixed attitudes and attributes of character. So far from the biologically fittest tending to survive, under modern war conditions these are the very ones who, for the most part and to the incalculable detriment of the future of the race, are killed off, even granting that of those who are "fit" enough to get to the front, the weakest are those who have the poorest chance of survival. And finally, when the stress of war conditions becomes acute, innumerable enterprises for social betterment are constrained to be given up, at least for the time being. In view, then, of all this, not to dwell upon the unspeakable suffering, physical and mental, on the part not only of combatants, but of non-combatants as well, and considering the merely problematical nature of the good to which the crisis involved in a state of war may prove a stimulus, it must be regarded as incredible that a God good enough and wise enough to be worthy of absolute dependence and worship could have ordered so stupendous a catastrophe as a possible means of human salvation. Neither is it reasonable to suppose that God is prolonging the war, in order that some social evils, such as drunkenness, may be eradicated before victory is finally secured. This might, perhaps, be the outcome, if the war were greatly prolonged; but it could not be at all certain beforehand that any such improvement would be permanent enough to offset the evils involved in the continuation of the war. We cannot suppose anyone who was wise enough and good enough to be God would be so far below our best human standards as to will either the existence or the continuation of the war as a whole, with all its attendant evils, in order that final good might abound. Any God who might be thought of as doing so would be a false God; his condemnation would be just.

Understanding, then, that in so far as human hatred, selfishness and stupidity have been factors in leading to the war, it has been originated, not by the will or in the providence of God, but against his will and providence; understanding also that in so far as it has been prolonged by human inefficiency or stupidity, or by the efficiency of evil wills, or of wills in the service of wrong, its continuation has not been in accordance with but in opposition to his will and providence, let us turn to the more positive aspect of the divine providence in connection with the war. It may be said to begin with, that in so far as going into this war has been correctly judged by any party to it to be the necessary alternative to national perfidy, or ignoble servitude, or any other evil greater than those involved in passing through the ordeal of war, and in so far as the task has been accepted as a solemn duty and entered upon in brave and self-sacrificing spirit, the act of going to war is to be regarded as in accord with the will of God. Indeed, if we may regard the divine spirit as immanent where we find the divine qualities present in human life, we may go further and say that such righteous participation in the war is the work of God within the soul of man, fighting against the forces of evil. Moreover, in so far as the war is prolonged by the fortitude of men of good intentions and their fidelity to a just cause, the war may similarly be said to be prolonged in accord with the will and even by the work of God in and through the good will and work of men.

But of providence in relation to the war as a whole, it can only be said that man's evil choice has compelled God to use the long, roundabout method. It is the second best method, although the best possible under the circumstances. The sinful choices of men and nations were not, of course, divinely predetermined. What has been divinely predetermined, we may well believe, is the law-abiding order of nature and of individual and social mind, according to which the disasters and sufferings incidental to war are the inevitable consequences of certain forms of individual and corporate wrong doing. In this roundabout way certain reforms may be providentially forced upon the nations by the war. The evil consequences of certain former evils tend to be more acutely felt under the strain and stress of severe and prolonged warfare.

Let us suppose that in order to win the war we and our Allies may yet find it necessary to take drastic steps to eradicate drunkenness with its attendant evils, or even to prohibit the waste of food-stuffs and fuel involved in the manufacture of alcoholic beverages. This would not mean that the war had been divinely caused in order to realize this end, but only that it was and always is the divine will that man should learn the lessons of the law of consequences, which lessons are in some instances more readily learned in time of war.

But what God is teaching most directly through the law of consequences in connection with the war is the necessity of correcting certain immoral international relations. He is teaching the nations through bitter experience how imperative are international righteousness and some practicable and adequately democratic scheme of world-government.

But we must not close our eyes to the possibility that through our failure to do our part, God may be forced to take the long, sad, roundabout way of exercising his providence in connection with the end, as he had to in the beginning of the war. What we must wake up to is this, that *in spite of the justice of our cause, in spite of its being the cause of humanity and in essential accord with the will of God, and in spite of our days of prayer and our optimistic religious faith,* GERMANY MAY WIN THIS WAR! If our consciousness of being right and our religious optimism make us so complacent that we shall fail to exert our utmost strength on behalf of our righteous cause, they may be the very factors that will turn the tide of war against us. We have resources enough for the winning of victory. If we fail it will be a moral failure. If we fail to rise to the moral demands of this great occasion, God may have to let us fail to win the war and then learn what we can from the bitter consequences of this failure. We and future generations may have to learn through tragic experience how imperative it is that right be not left to enforce itself, but that we devote our full might to the cause of right, and that before it is too late.

At the time of writing these words—in the early days of May, 1918—it seems not yet too late, however critical the situation, for the winning of victory for the cause of liberty and justice. But the surest way of providing for success would be for all who recognize the right so to surrender themselves to the will of God for self-sacrificing service, and so to depend upon the indwelling power of God for inner preparedness for whatever may have to be faced and whatever may have to be done, that their whole might may be made use of in this warfare for the right. Our primary need is *morale*—morale in the government, morale in the shipyards, morale in the munitions factories, morale among all our people in their business and home life, as well as fighting spirit in our army and navy abroad. Enough religion of the right sort may make enough difference in morale to make all the difference between defeat and victory as the outcome of this war. And if in this way victory for the right should come as a result of religion, it would be not only a crowning example of the short and preferred method of divine providence; it would be, literally speaking, victory by the Grace of God.

In any case, the situation for the Western Allies is such that neither faith without works nor works without faith can accomplish what waits to be done. There must be, if we would win, faith and works together.

Before leaving this topic of God and history, a word may be said on the question of what, on this interpretation of providence, we may expect to be the final outcome of this war for the future of the race. Will the result be more harm than good, or more good than harm? It is very certain that the war will need to be the occasion of an immense amount of good to balance up to the race the evils that have been involved in it thus far and that will be involved in its prolongation. Much possible evil will be avoided if the immoral Prussian militaristic ideal is finally crushed. Moreover, there will be the tendency for humanity to learn, at least temporarily and as an intellectual conviction, the undesirability of war and of the conditions that make for war. But attention and moral effort will be necessary to retain this lesson with sufficient impressiveness, and to put it into effect, and the best power of thought will be needed to determine just how this putting it into effect may be most fully and lastingly secured. There seems real danger that the human race on earth will be permanently poorer and worse off, spiritually and socially as well as biologically and economically, as a result of this nearest approach to racial suicide. Undoubtedly it will be so, if the nations fail to learn and to put into effect the lesson of the necessity of international righteousness and a just and efficient system of world-government.

It is perhaps still possible for the race to learn enough from this period of strife and carnage for the resultant good to outbalance the total evil. But even then no one would have the right to credit the war with having been the means of greater good than *could* have been accomplished without it. All its moral evil at any rate will be regrettable forever. And the only possible way of guaranteeing beforehand greater good than evil as an outcome of the war, even supposing the side of justice and liberty to be victorious, will be for individuals and groups so to relate themselves to truth, to right and to God that flagrantly immoral international relations will become practically impossible. The only safety of the race lies in an essentially Christian international morality, and the only adequate guarantee of this is an essentially Christian personal religion. The only failure of essential Christianity of which the war may fairly be regarded as evidence was its failure to be given an adequate trial; which means, of course, not a failure of Christianity as an ethical or as a religious system, but a failure of the human will to be adequately Christian.

III

THE CHRISTIAN HOPE IN TIMES OF WAR

FRANK CHAMBERLIN PORTER

Of Paul's three things that abide, hope is the one of which we are now most conscious of our need. Never before in our experience has hope been so much the center of our inner life and the heart of our religion. Our mood alternates between hope and depression, hope and fear; and we look to our religion to make hope strong, and turn to our sacred book to seek secure grounds and satisfying expressions for our hope. We hope for the winning of the war. We hope for the safety and the home-coming of those we love. We hope for a new world-order organized to make war impossible, inspired by a spirit of coöperation and good will between classes and between nations. We hope as never before for an assured and abundant life after death. We put these hopes in some relation to each other, weighing one against another, subordinating one to another. And when we seek their right relationship and look for their ultimate grounds, we ask what Christianity has to say and to do about them. What is Christian in these hopes that are filling the mind and heart of the world? The importance of this question is very great. The future of the world depends on the truth and the strength of the hopes that now inspire and direct men's purposes and efforts. The future of the Christian religion turns in no small measure on its ability now to keep the hope of mankind high and pure, free from self-seeking and from material interests, and true to the ultimate reality of things, and to give this hope confidence and prevailing strength.

Christians are not at one over the question what, as Christians, they have a right to hope for. Most evidently is this the case between us and our enemy. We differ in things hoped for; and it is perhaps not too much to say that the truth of our hope and the strength of our hope constitute and measure our spiritual equipment for the winning of the war. The Germans are fighting for their hope of national expansion and domination, for their dream of a new world empire of the chosen and fit people of God. We cannot question the strength of this hope of theirs, and its powerful influence toward bringing itself to realization. We and our Allies are resisting these nationalistic and arrogant hopes, and are appealing to the contrary hope of an inclusive human brotherhood, in which good will shall prevail between nations, and hence right and peace. The hope that is truer, more in accordance with the nature of things, the nature of man, the will of God, and the hope that is most deeply felt and most loyally served, with most conviction and most sacrifice, will prevail in the end. That is the hope that will come true. Ours is inevitably a religious hope, for it is universal in range, big as the world, and needs not only every power of ours but the Power not ourselves to bring it about. It is for every one who holds it intensely, in a real sense, a hope in God and a hope for God. But is it certain that it is also a Christian hope, a hope in Christ and a hope for Christ?

There are, not only between us and our enemy, but among ourselves, radical differences as to what a Christian should hope for in the present world crisis. There are those who search the Scriptures for predictions of the Kaiser and his overthrow, and see in the anti-Christian philosophy and in the anti-Christian arrogance and cruelty of his militaristic state, a sign that the end of this evil world-age is near, and that Christ will come quickly and set up his reign on earth. And there are those to whom such literalism in the use of Scripture and such externality in the hope for Christ's coming are intellectually impossible and untrue, and religiously harmful. To them the meaning of the Bible is to be found in the tendency and spirit of its teachings, and their hope is for the presence and rule of the spirit of Christ and the dominance of his principles in the common life of humanity. This involves a radical difference in the hope of Christians for a new world, a new human society, and in the ways in which this hope will affect their motives and efforts. There are also deep-going differences in regard to the hope for a life after death. That many are looking eagerly for material, "scientific" proof through physical communications from the dead, while many, on the other hand, are feeling that immortality belongs to the race and not to the individual, and that the sacrifice of the young and the strong finds its only and sufficient end and justification in the new humanity they die to create, indicates that Christ has not yet brought life and immortality to clear light for humanity. Such differences are not to be desired. If Christianity is to be the religion of the present eager and pressing hopes of mankind and give these hopes elevation, truth, and victorious endurance and enthusiasm, Christians should be clear and united in the contents and character of their hope.

Among these hopes of mankind there can be no doubt which one has the first place in the minds of the intellectual leaders and the actual rulers of the allied nations. Never before has a truly prophetic note been so clearly sounded by leading men of affairs, and by the press and the leaders of public opinion, as well as by the poets and preachers to whom prophecy naturally belongs. From all sides we have expressions of a hope which four years ago was judged to be the dream of impractical idealists, the hope for a new order of human life, in which good will and mutual coöperation shall take the place of suspicion and competitive struggle. We need not be blind to whatever motives of self-interest may have entered into the action of this or that one of our Allies in undertaking the war. The outstanding fact remains that while the German Government appeals to the self-assertion of the German State and seeks its aggrandizement through force at the expense of its neighbors, the allied governments appeal to national self-sacrifice for the sake of international redemption. It is to this appeal on behalf of the rights, the freedom, the happiness of mankind, that our soldiers respond; for humanity, not for national gain, that our peoples are prepared to give and to suffer. This hope takes concrete form in the word Democracy, and in the idea of a League or Federation of free, democratic nations, bound together for the defense of human rights, for coöperation in all that concerns human welfare and progress, and the repression of every attack upon the peace of the world. So viewed the war becomes definitely a war to end war, and as such it is engaged in and supported by peace-loving peoples, against the nation that glorifies war and would perpetuate it.

Is this great hope Christian? Is Christianity the religion which a hope so high and so difficult needs if it is to keep its height amid the many influences that tend to lower it, and if it is to prove possible and become actual in spite of powerful forces that work against it? It is not self-evident that Christianity will prove equal to this which is clearly the greatest task that the present imposes upon it. There are many who doubt its adequacy; many who see that it has brought division and warfare, and think it unfitted to create unity; many who see that it has withdrawn from the world, and think it unadapted to provide the moral principles and spiritual energies of the new social and political world-order. It is for us who believe in the sufficiency of Christ to prove that he alone provides those religious and moral principles and forces without which no democracy, still less any federation of democracies, can stand.

The ideal of human brotherhood which the war has revealed as the deepest desire and faith of men and has put before us as a goal that we must now set out to reach is of course old in its beginnings, and for a generation it has been taking ever stronger hold on the minds of men. Prophetic utterances of this ideal could be quoted in abundance. A striking example is a saying of Alexander Dumas in 1893: "I believe our world is about to begin to realize the words 'Love one another,' without, however, being concerned whether a man or a God uttered them. . . . Mankind, which does nothing moderately, is about to be seized with a frenzy, a madness, of love." And Tolstoy's comment on this at the time of the Russian revolution, in 1905: "I believe that this thought, however strange the expression, 'seized with a frenzy of love,' may seem, is perfectly true and is felt more or less clearly by all men of our day. A time must come when love, which forms the fundamental essence of the soul, will take the place natural to it in the life of mankind, and will become the chief basis of the relations between man and man. That time is coming; it is at hand."

The world war seems like a violent contradiction of the truth of such prophecies. It seems for the time to have made love inadequate as a summing up of morals and religion. We almost feel that the Sermon on the Mount must be kept in reserve for other times. The war has made love itself a hope. We renounce it for a time that we may resist a power that threatens to destroy it altogether and put selfishness and cruelty on the throne of the world. But the war has not in fact disproved the faith that God is love and that love is the supreme law and power among men. It has made mankind more conscious of its ideal of community and fellowship, and seems to be carrying us faster toward the realization of human brotherhood than peace and prosperity were doing. The greatest and most widely approved sentences of President Wilson's war papers are those that give expression to "what the thinking peoples of the world desire, with their longing hope for justice and for social freedom and opportunity." On the anniversary of our entering the war, Gilbert Murray declared that England needed our help in battle, but even more in upholding their true faith. "Americans instinctively believe . . . in freedom, peace, democracy, arbitration, and international good will. . . . When the war is over there will be a world to rebuild, and the only principles on which to rebuild it are these principles." Germany denies the truth of these principles, but in doing so it denies human nature and derives from physical nature a state-ethics of struggle and the survival of the strong. It denies the prophet of Galilee, and looks for its example to Rome. Sometimes it has seemed as if the German denial of humanity and affirmation of material and brute force were in danger of justifying itself by the only test they admit, that of physical success. Where can we look for help toward a living faith in liberty and brotherhood over against the powerful demonstration we are offered of faith in material force and in the progress of nations through aggression and tyranny? We must look no doubt first of all to our own souls and oppose to the faith in physical and animal nature a faith in human nature and in the truth of its best instincts and ideals; and then to those who know best and most worthily express the human soul and the reality of its spiritual possessions. Not from the Bible alone, and not only from Christ are such reassuring testimonies to be gained; and we are not renouncing the unique value of the Christian religion when we find that the faith and hope which it teaches are the faith and the hope of the universal heart of man.

The poet laureate of England made his special contribution to his nation's needs in time of war in the anthology, "The Spirit of Man." "Our country," he says, "is called of God to stand for the truth of man's hope." "Truly it is the hope of man's great desire, the desire for brotherhood and universal peace to men of good will, that is at stake in this struggle." From the miseries and slaughter and hate of war, "we can turn," he says, "to seek comfort only in the quiet confidence of our souls; and we look instinctively to the seers and poets of mankind, whose sayings are the oracles and prophecies of loveliness and loving kindness." They help us gain the conviction our time most needs, "that spirituality is the basis and foundation of human life," that "man is a spiritual being, and the proper work of his mind is to interpret the world according to his higher nature, and to conquer the material aspects of the world so as to bring them into submission to the spirit."

But the Bible also is a witness to just these convictions and contains prophecies of just such hopes. Bridges includes very few citations from the Bible, chiefly because it is so well known, but also because "this familiarity implies deep-rooted associations, which would be likely to distort the context." Alas, for these associations, for the interpretations that confuse and the prejudices that blind the readers of the greatest literature of spirituality and of hope which the world contains. In spite of this, the Bible will be looked to by multitudes for guidance and support in those hopes on which the future turns, while the poet's fine work will be prized by few. It is only too possible to fail to find in the Bible its testimony to that "hope of man's great desire of brotherhood and peace" which constitutes the most living religion of our time; and this failure will mean loss to the hope itself of its most powerful support, and loss to the Christian religion of contact and sympathy with the most urgent spiritual need and aspiration of men to-day.

The Bible does contain various and contradictory hopes, and can encourage expectations that are not in accordance with the best conscience of our age, nor with our knowledge of the way in which human progress is achieved. But there is nothing more instructive than the relation of these different hopes to each other as the historian understands them and there is nothing more worthy and inspiring than the language in which the most spiritual and the most universal of these hopes are expressed.

The original hope of the religion of Israel was that involved in the unique and exclusive relation between the nation Israel and Yahweh, its God. It was the hope of Israel's prosperity and power through the certain favor of Yahweh, and his intervening help in times of danger, most of all his help in the nation's wars. These were "the Wars of Yahweh." Both the strength and the defect of the Old Testament religion lie in this fundamental faith, the peculiarity and exclusiveness of the relation between Israel and its God. It inspired its early victories and created the kingdom of David. It sustained the nation amid calamities and enabled it to maintain itself when other small nations disappeared before the great world empires, and while these also came and passed. It was a natural and not unreasonable faith for its time, so long as Yahweh was only Israel's national God, even though he was believed to be better and stronger than the gods of other nations and destined to triumph over them; but when Israel's God was believed to be the one and only God of all the world the doctrine of Israel as his peculiar people must either lead to false claims and have bad effects upon temper and conduct, or else be reinterpreted and radically changed. Nothing can be more instructive as to the nature of religious hope than to follow out two main lines of development by which an adjustment was attempted between this primitive nationalism and the later, larger thought of God and the world.

The great prophets before the exile, Amos, Hosea, Isaiah, Jeremiah, and after exile Deutero-Isaiah, were those through whom the faith was attained that Yahweh is the one and only God; and the modification of the national exclusiveness of Israel which they made was in the direction of its complete subordination to ethical and spiritual ideals. The one God of all was the God of righteousness, and of Israel only on the condition and for the end of righteousness. But an ethical in place of a national relation to God meant, if it was carried through consistently, a universal relation of God to all men as individuals, instead of a peculiar relation to one favored nation. Consistency was not reached, yet glimpses, sometimes clear momentary visions, of this individual, universal, ethical religion are to be found in the great prophets; and in them the Old Testament religion reaches its height. It is the prophetic denial of national claims and hopes, not the older and always prevalent assertion of them, that constitutes the reality and truth of the Old Testament hope. It is hope for Yahweh and his righteousness, not for Israel and its glory. It finds its highest expression in such predictions as Isaiah's promise of security to the humble and believing; and Jeremiah's expectation of the time when no special revelation will make known the will of God to a chosen few, but when everyone will have his own inward knowledge of God; and Ezekiel's belief that the new inward nature which every man requires if he is to do that will of God which he knows, will be achieved not only by his own free moral choice (18:31), but also by the divine spirit, the transforming presence and power of God (36:26, 27); and in Deutero-Isaiah's interpretation of the peculiar relation of Israel to the one God of all the world as that of Yahweh's Servant, his prophet to all nations, who brings light to the heathen and deliverance from bondage, and who effects this ministry even through his own shame and suffering for others' sins.

But there was a second still later way of adjusting the original nationalism of Israel's faith and hope to monotheism and the conception of a unity in nature and history; and this proved easier and more popular than the other. In late prophecy and apocalypse the hope of Israel's national and worldly prosperity and power takes on an unearthly character. Instead of righteousness and spirituality as in the earlier prophets, transcendence and heavenliness interpret or displace the primitive hope. The heavenly region to which apocalyptic prophecy transferred Israel's hope was a refinement of the physical, but it was still essentially physical, a region whose riches could be as sensibly enjoyed and as selfishly desired as the palace and throne of an earthly kingdom. The heavenly powers by which this hope was to be realized were divine, yet they were essentially material forces. The prophetic hopes at their highest rest on human nature at its highest, on the conscience and reason of man recognized as the will and thought of God. But the apocalyptic hope, though it strains language to magnify the contrast between its two worlds, the earthly and the heavenly, the present and the future, does not succeed in making them really different. Supernaturalism always fails to find the real difference between man and God and so the way in which the difference is to be overcome. This supernaturalism of the apocalypse is seen also in the ways in which the hope is revealed. The seer interprets in literal or artful ways the language of prophetic scriptures regarded as divine oracles, or he is translated in ecstasy to heaven and shown the secrets of the upper world and the future. The coming of this new heavenly world men may pray for, and the time of its coming they may seek to discover from sacred writings and traditions and from the signs of the times, but only divine powers can bring this evil world to an end, and only from heaven where they already are can descend, in heaven's own time and way, the scenery and the actors in the last great drama of history. There is in this hope no strong ethical appeal, no prevailing sense that in the inward region of the heart and in its instincts and desires and wills, God's presence is to be found and his work for man experienced. Moreover this hope for a new heavenly world means no hope for the present world. It is evil and must grow more evil until God intervenes to destroy it and brings down from heaven the realm of good. To renounce the world and withdraw from it is the course of wisdom and holiness. As a way of adjusting Israel's national hope to monotheism it is not comparable with the prophetic way of ethics and inwardness. It is still Israel, or the true Israel, that is to inherit the world to come; and at its coming the world empire must first of all be overthrown, for the new kingdom, heavenly and supernatural though it is, is enough like the kingdom of Greece or of Rome to require its fall and to take its place. The apocalyptic hope is the end of Old Testament prophecy, but not its height. It was no doubt in some sense fitted for its times, hard times, always, when the evils of life seemed irremediable. It knew the need of divine help, and it encouraged endurance and fidelity even to death. But it was not grounded in the nature of men, and it was mistaken in its conception of the nature of the world. It never quite escapes this inherent falseness and confusion in its fundamental assumptions.

It cannot be hard to pass judgment on the relative value of these three main hopes of the Old Testament. The primitive hope for God's special favor to his own peculiar people who are destined to have dominion over all others would have seemed, before the war, safely outgrown by humanity. If the world still needed a demonstration of the danger and falsity of any nation's belief in its peculiar excellence and in its exclusive right and destiny to rule, and the intolerable morals and preposterous religion that finally result from such claims, the aggressors in the present war have supplied it, and the rest of the world is united in the resolve that no further demonstration of this hope be undertaken. The early histories of the Old Testament and parts of its laws, its psalms and even its prophecies, contain expressions of just this belief in a peculiar people, for whom God made the world, and to whom the right belongs, secured by the divine favor and promise, to rule over all other nations. Some of the inferences and consequences of this faith that now shock the world, something of the hatred and the cruelty toward foreign peoples, the exaltation of vengeance, the arrogance and the inhumanity, find unreserved expression in this literature. But the meaning of the Old Testament is to be found in the denial and overcoming of this doctrine and of its results.

In regard to the two ways in which this denial and correction were chiefly undertaken, there can be no question where the greater value and truth are to be found. The prophet's criticism of the national hope and reinterpretation of it as the hope for righteousness really struck at the heart of the materialism and selfishness of the popular national hope, its false pride and its denial of trust and of good will toward mankind. But the apocalyptic modification of the older hope, though it fitted it for a wider view of the world and of history and a deeper experience of the power of evil, did not correct those moral and spiritual faults which were inherent in the older hope. There is no generosity, no faith in human nature, no sense of the present prevailing rule of God and power of good, no thought of the "secret of inwardness" and "the method of self-renouncement," in the religion of the apocalypse. The righteous kernel of Judaism, the holy few who feared the Lord, expected an invasion of divine forces on their behalf, the destruction of their oppressors and their own elevation to angel-like natures and God-like authority and blessedness. It could hardly be expected that they would exhibit Isaiah's virtue of humility, or Jeremiah's of inwardness and satisfaction in the communion of the soul with God, or Deutero-Isaiah's impulse to turn their present lowliness to greatness by ministry to those who persecuted them and even by death for others' transgressions. The greatest of the apocalypses are no doubt the canonical ones, Daniel and Revelation; and they are great in their confidence in the divine government of the world, and in its final vindication, and in their assertion of the martyr virtues. But they do not believe in man, and in God in man, though their belief in a God above is heroic. They do not hope for the world, or find God in the world; nor do they feel that they are in any sense responsible for the evil of the world and for its salvation from evil. Righteousness and blessedness belong only to heaven, and can come only from heaven to earth, and only by an act of God which will bring the present world to a sudden end. The faults of materialism and of self-interest which belong to the naïve nationalism of Israel's beginnings are still present in the conscious and sophisticated other-worldliness of the apocalyptic hopes, and reveal the inner untruth of a supernaturalism which reckons in terms of place and time, and looks above and ahead instead of about and within for the Kingdom of God.

The post-canonical apocalypses of Judaism fall within the

period beginning with the attempt of Antiochus IV to make the Jews Greeks, and the successful resistance of the Maccabees and their establishment of an independent Jewish kingdom, and ending with the Jewish-Roman wars, the destruction of Jerusalem and the suppression by Hadrian of the final Messianic, political uprising under Bar Cochba; that is, from 168 B. C. to 135 A. D. It is of the highest importance to note that Christianity took its rise in the midst of this period, and that the apocalyptic hopes which these events encouraged and which in turn partly shaped the events, formed the immediate environment and inheritance of the new religion. The question as to the nature of the hope of the New Testament becomes therefore largely the question of the place which Jewish apocalyptical expectations had in the new religion and in the mind of its founder.

There are three elements in the hope of the New Testament which are found in the later Jewish apocalypses, but not in the Old Testament: 1. The coming of the Son of Man as judge of men and angels at the last day, which is always thought to be near at hand. 2. The reign on earth of Messiah and his saints, the living and the risen dead, for a certain period, during which they will overcome all the powers of evil. 3. The immortality of the spirit, the transformation of the righteous into angelic natures, fitting them to be companions of heavenly beings in the final consummation. For our understanding of these hopes and for our decision as to their truth and value it is necessary to look at them as they arise in Jewish writings and not only in their appearance in the New Testament.

The Son of Man appears first in Daniel, but there he is not an individual, but the symbol of a nation, "the people of the saints of the Most High"; and the vision pictures Israel as coming on a cloud, not from heaven, but to God, to receive from him authority to rule over the world. It is first in a part of the Book of Enoch, the "Parables," chapters 37-71, dating probably from the reign of Herod, that Daniel's "Son of Man" becomes an individual. It is important to understand the religion of this writer in order to appreciate the significance of this heavenly Messiah. His religion consists in faith in the reality of a spiritual world which is destined to displace the present world and to be the blessed abode of the righteous. God is "the Lord of Spirits," and the voice of Isaiah's seraphim becomes, "Holy, holy, holy, is the Lord of Spirits: he filleth the earth with spirits." The sin of the kings and mighty of the earth is that they deny the Lord of Spirits and the hidden dwelling places of the righteous. This is a religion of faith in heaven and its God and its angelic inhabitants, and in the destiny of the righteous soon to share its beauty and blessedness. Among those whom Enoch sees there, one is above all significant for man. He has the appearance of a man, with a face of graciousness and beauty, like an angel's. He is described as the Son of Man to whom righteousness and wisdom belong. He has existed from before the creation, and has been revealed to the righteous. Faith in him and hope for his coming have sustained the righteous in times of trouble, and by faith in him and in the Lord of Spirits and the heavenly dwelling places, they "have hated and despised the world of unrighteousness and have hated all its works and ways." Here is a religion of pure other-worldliness. The calling of this heavenly Son of Man is to be the judge of the world at the last day. He will then "sit on the throne of his glory," will "choose the righteous and holy" from among the risen dead, will condemn and send away to destruction the kings and mighty of the earth, who because of their unbelief in the unseen world have been proud and worldly and unjust. The righteous will dwell in the new heaven and earth, with the Lord of Spirits over them and the Son of Man as their companion, having been clothed with garments of glory and immortal life. The likeness between this religion and the apocalyptic type of New Testament Christianity is striking. But it is not Christian because it is without Jesus himself. This Son of Man has not already come and lived among men. The righteous have not learned of him that God is in this world as well as in the other, that he is a God of human beings, even the lowliest, and of birds and grass, of rain and growth. They have not learned that good is already stronger than evil; least of all do they know the greatest thing, that love is supreme, and that not by hating the world and its ways but by the ministry of love is the new world to be brought in. The religion of Enoch presents in pure and simple form, in pre-Christian Judaism, just that religion of dualism and pessimism, of despair of the present and the renunciation of effort to better the world, of strained expectation of divine intervention, which sometimes, and even now in some quarters, claims to be the only true Christianity. It is, in fact, Christianity with Christ left out.

The second element which the apocalypses add to the hope of the Old Testament and which the New Testament Apocalypse adopts, is the conception of a millennial earthly kingdom. This appears in probably an earlier part of Enoch, chapters 91-104. In a short Apocalypse of Weeks, after seven weeks of world-history up to the writer's present, an eighth week is predicted, in which the righteous shall wield the sword against their oppressors and establish the Messianic kingdom; then a ninth week in which the preaching of judgment to come will convert all men to righteousness; finally, a tenth week of final judgment against all angelic powers of evil, ending with a new heaven and an eternity of blessedness.

It is not only the fact that here and elsewhere these two hopes are proved to be Jewish, not Christian, in origin, that influences our judgment on them when they reappear in the New Testament; it is also the understanding of them which their Jewish form makes possible. They are two forms of adjusting the old national and earthly hope of Israel to a new, more universal and transcendent form of faith and hope. In the religion of the "Parables" of Enoch the transcendent practically transforms and displaces the earthly. In the millennial scheme, the heavenly follows the earthly in time. Resurrection enables some of the dead to have part in the earthly, while translation into angel-like, immortal natures fits men for the final heavenly life. The understanding of the origin and purpose of these hopes makes it unnatural and irrational to regard them as literal disclosures of the unseen world and of future events.

The third hope which Judaism added to what its sacred scriptures contained was the hope for immortality of the spirit. It happens that this also appears earliest in Judaism in the Book of Enoch (especially chapters 102-104). Enoch solemnly assures his readers that he has seen it written in heavenly books that joy and glory are prepared for the spirits of those who have died in righteousness. This is not a resurrection of the body to enable one to have a share in the earthly kingdom, but a transformation which fits men for the realm of spirits.

When we turn in the light of the older hopes to the New Testament and ask what are the hopes that belong properly to Christianity, and how are they related to the present hopes of the world, we meet the problem presented by the importance of properly apocalyptical expectations in the first Christian community. The case is something like that which meets us in the Old Testament, and we have here no less than there to distinguish and to choose. The hope of the early Christian community was no doubt first of all for the physical coming of Christ and the establishment of his kingdom; but there developed also within the New Testament period two movements away from this, one in an ethical and spiritual direction, and the other toward emphasis on the individual life after death. The first of these is more characteristic of the New Testament religion than the other. It is the tendency of Paul to emphasize the present inward experience of Christ, and the transforming power of his spirit more than the hope of his coming, though he receives this from primitive Christianity and does not doubt its literal and early fulfilment. It is, I believe, beyond question that Paul's Christian hope is chiefly, as Royce has argued, the hope for a new humanity created by the spirit of Christ, which is the spirit of love. This is in a measure already experienced. Christ dwells in the Christian and makes him a center and source of love. His spirit breaks down barriers and ends divisions. Unity and peace are its effects. Through this one, present spirit of Christ each man becomes a distinct but essential member of the new body; and Paul's greatest hope is for the completion of this unification of man in mutual helpfulness and brotherhood. Paul attests also the other tendency away from the outward future coming of Christ to the hope for a life with Christ and like Christ's after death. This eternal life with Christ is also experienced by Paul as in some real sense present. The indwelling spirit of Christ is already transforming the Christian into his own immortal nature. In the Johannine writings these two tendencies of hope away from the apocalyptic toward the spiritual go still further. The Christ in whom the Christian now abides creates a distinctive unity among his disciples, a love one to another which the world has not known; and at the same time the experience of this present Christ is already the possession of eternal life. According to this which we might call the prophetic in distinction from the apocalyptic hope of the New Testament the new world of human unity in love and coöperation is to be brought about not only by the present spirit of Christ, but also by the moral choice and endeavor of man. It is through human love that the divine love works, and the rule of God is present so far as men overcome evil and create good. And even the immortal life is not solely a hope in God, but is to be attained by each soul here and now through its choice of the will of God and in the degree of its moral oneness with God.

That which most concerns us is no doubt the question which of these hopes, the eschatological or the ethical and inward, was held and taught by Christ. My own conviction is that the new and distinct hope, the spiritual, belongs to him and proceeds from him, and not the familiar Jewish apocalyptic. Two opinions stand in the way of this judgment; two opposite types of literalism in Biblical interpretation. Dogmatic literalism accepts scripture throughout, and refuses to distinguish between higher and lower, between truth and error, in what is written. In regard to hope, this view leads to great stress on prediction and fulfilment. The assumption is that the Biblical predictions that have not been fulfilled will come to pass in the future. This is precisely a fundamental assumption of the apocalypse. It is solely upon this conception of scripture that many devout Christians rest their expectations of the outward coming of Christ and his thousand-year reign on earth, just as the same idea of Biblical predictions leads orthodox Jews to expect that Jerusalem will be the capital and Israel the ruling nation of the world. This literalism stands in the way of the world's present acceptance of Christianity as the religion of its highest hopes.

But there is a like danger in the opposite literalism of the historian. We have already seen how the history of Jewish hopes makes the literal acceptance of similar New Testament hopes unnatural if not impossible. The literalism of the historian is, of course, to us true and immediately helpful in liberating us from bondage to the letter of an ancient book. It leaves us free to apply our own reason and conscience and experience to the interpretation of our own life and times. It turns us back upon our own souls, upon our faith, our desire, our will, to unveil and shape the future. But the historian is in danger of doing less than justice to the ethical and spiritual contents of the hopes of the Bible because of his very love of truth and willingness to sacrifice his wishes to it. The unpardonable sin to him is the modernizing of an ancient writing because of reverence for it, and the effort to find in it what he likes rather than things outgrown and unwelcome. This conscientious fear, I cannot but believe, has resulted in a one-sided interpretation of the New Testament, especially the teachings of Jesus and of Paul, as essentially apocalyptic in contents and spirit, and a hesitation to recognize the essentially inward, rational and ethical quality, the prophetic character of the New Testament as a whole, and to make due allowance for the ease and naturalness with which the current apocalyptic ideas of early Jewish Christians could persist and be applied to Jesus and attributed to him.

This problem over which New Testament scholars are divided into two groups or tendencies is of course much too complicated to discuss here. But it is necessary at least to point out that there is a danger in the historian's anxiety to be without prejudice, and to view the past as past. The greatness of great men and great books is to be found in the eternal meaning, not in the mere form, of what they say. Historians no less than other men have the right and duty to ask in what direction an ancient teacher is looking, toward what goal the movement of his mind is tending, what final effects he produced, what therefore he would think and say if he lived in our time. We are told that it is unhistorical to seek in the New Testament for "the modern liberal Christ"; but it is not unhistorical to look for the human beneath the Jewish, the eternal and universal within the temporary and limited. The mind of Christ, his manner and mood, his quality, his spirit, is not less a historical reality than his literal words. This is of course true also of Paul, and, in his measure, of every man.

There can be no doubt that like the great prophets before him Jesus was chiefly a critic and corrector of the hopes of his time. He did not approve the national hopes that had been kindled by the Maccabean kingdom and were soon to issue in the suicidal revolt against Rome. Whether Jesus expected the speedy coming of the Son of Man and the end of the world, and whether he identified himself with this transcendent Messiah-Judge, are questions made difficult, not by our wishes, but by the nature of the evidence. My own inclination is, at this point, to attribute more to the influence of Jewish expectations on the gospel traditions than to Jesus' own words. What seems to me certain is that the bearing of the teaching of Jesus was in the direction of the spiritual hopes of Paul and John rather than the apocalyptic hopes which they still held in common with the first disciples.

It is the fundamental principle of the apocalyptic hope that God made not one world but two (II Esdras 7:50). This world must end and the other world must come if evil is to end and good prevail. But Jesus believed that this world is already God's world, and that in it good is already stronger than evil. The Kingdom of God is indeed still to come, but it is already within. It is already upon us when by the spirit of God evil is cast out. It has been said that it was the Greeks who believed in one world in contrast to the Jews who believed in two; and that Poseidonius, the Platonic Stoic, an oriental, of the century before Christ, wrote to make men at home in the universe. But it is surely not a mistake to say that Jesus felt at home in the world and meant to make others at home. This is precisely the meaning of the word Father, of which Paul testifies that Jesus' use was to a Jew new, and that it meant freedom from mental bondage and fear. Poseidonius made men feel at home in the universe by denying the existence of evil, which is of course one way of making one world out of two; Jesus by affirming the reality of a goodness in God and in man capable of conquering evil. That God is Father, the Father of all men, even, and especially, of sinners, is not the basis of an apocalyptic hope. Jesus did not chiefly foretell the end of the world through the catastrophic intervention of God or of the Son of Man. He did chiefly teach that the power not ourselves is fatherly, that it is human, that we can trust our own souls at their best to teach us the nature of God, that our highest human values are the ultimate realities of the universe. Jesus found that the chief fears and hopes of men were concerned with bodily welfare and possessions and with power over others. Mammon and dominion were the false gods men worshipped. Wealth and power seem now the objects of the hope and the religious devotion of the Central Powers. Jesus declared that it is the heathen who are anxious about food and raiment. It is the heathen who lord it over their fellow men. Not so was it to be among his disciples. Since the Father knows our needs and wills to give good things, since the outer world belongs to him and since the things of the soul are of the greater value, we men are free to put first things first, to seek God's Kingdom and righteousness. And since God's rule consists in love and in doing good, without reserve or regard for deserts or for returns, the only real rulership among men also must be the renunciation of rulership for the sake of ministry. Not to be masters over others, not to be strong by making others weak, but to serve and to give is the divine plan, the real nature of things. This is not what the war lords learn from physical and animal nature as to the way to success and primacy, but it is true to that human nature to which they do violence. The Christian hope is therefore not for material possessions nor for authority and power; it is that spiritual realities shall vindicate and make effectual their preëminence, and shall master matter and all outward things for their own ends; and that unselfish love shall measure greatness among men and shall destroy hatred and fear and create a human family.

If this, according to Christ, is the Christian hope, then Christianity is certainly the religion for the present hope of the world. The hope of a league of free nations, of a federated world in which democracy is safe, is clearly seen by those who see best what it involves and what obstacles stand in its way to be first of all the hope for a new spirit among men, a new inward temper, a new will; it is also seen to be something universal in its range. Not again one league against another, but a league that at least aims at being inclusive of humanity. Spirituality and universality, inwardness and good-will, belong to the hope that is now inspiring the nations; and these are just the marks of the religion of Christ; they are what Matthew Arnold called the method of inwardness and the secret of self-renouncement, controlled by the mildness and sweet reasonableness of Christ; reverence for the soul, meaning both the preëminent worth of every individual and the primacy in each of the things of the soul; and among these the chief greatness and God-likeness of love. However one attempts to sum up the religion of Jesus it is sure to mean in the end the same two things which the world now sees to be its great needs and the ground and heart of its hope.

It would be tragic indeed if Christianity should lose its supreme opportunity by failing to lead and inspire this newly emerging and Christ-like hope of men. It can fail if it confuses itself in the details of Biblical predictions, if it becomes involved in apocalyptic fancies. It can fail if in reaction against these and under the influence of an equally literalistic criticism men turn from the Bible altogether as a book of the past.

The men of our time are shaping the hope of a united and friendly human family of free peoples, united not only against war but for all kinds of mutual help and coöperative progress; and the Bible, the prophets of the Old Testament, Jesus and Paul in the New, are the chief creative sources of just such hopes. These hopes must have religion beneath them if they are to endure and be realized in spite of their powerful foes, the fears and hatreds which materialism and selfishness create. And Christianity is the only religion which has the quality and the right to meet this need.

The Christian hope is also the hope of immortality; and just now the reality and power of this hope are put to the test. Paul, who knew how far Judaism had gone toward faith in the eternal life of the spirit, testifies that it was only as a Christian and because of Christ that this hope had become to him a certainty, almost a present experience. The nature of God as Christ knew him, and the nature of man's sonship to God, carry immortality with them as an inward and immediate assurance. God is not the God of the dead, but of the living. Here again the Christian religion has an opportunity and an obligation in times of war. Men are seeking assurance of life to come for those who have given their lives for human right and liberty. It is not to be desired that this pressing religious need of our day should turn to physical evidences, to messages from the dead through abnormal experiences and dubious agencies. The Christian faith in immortality is to be experienced as faith in the God who loves as a father, and who gives as love must give his best to his children. If God is love, then our love does not deceive us. If God is spirit, then our spirits are from God and will return to him. If the soul, the person, is of supreme worth and reality, then it will not be involved in the body's destruction, nor lost as a drop in the ocean or as a breath in the wind, either in the divine being from whom it came, or in the human race, "the beloved community," to which its service is given.

It is perhaps in the relation to each other of the hope for a new human brotherhood and the hope for the life of the soul with God, that the distinction and preëminence of the religion of Jesus come most clearly to light. He feels no need of sacrificing one to the other, but holds his hope for this world and the oneness of men in love side by side with the hope for the other world. He does call upon individuals to give their lives in ministry to others, but in the losing of life he declares that life is gained. Paradoxes express his faith and insight, and the nature of love in God and in man brings with it the key to the solution of the paradox.

The Christian hopes for a new human brotherhood on earth and for the immortality of the individual are involved, and their principles given, in the simple and profound sayings of Jesus, and no other testimony as to their nature and certainty can be compared with his. To no other words is the response of our own spirits so instant and sure. Blessed are the poor in spirit, the meek, the merciful, the pure in heart: theirs is the kingdom of heaven; they shall see God. Love your enemies, that ye may be sons of your Father. Ye shall be perfect as your heavenly Father is perfect. Lay not up for yourselves treasures upon earth. Ye cannot serve God and mammon. Be not anxious for your life what ye shall eat or what ye shall drink, nor yet for your body what ye shall put on. Is not the life more than food and the body than raiment? Behold the birds of the heaven . . . Are not ye of much more value than they? Your Father knoweth that ye have need of all these things. But seek ye his kingdom and righteousness. Be not afraid of them that kill the body. The very hairs of your head are all numbered. Fear not therefore. If ye being evil know how to give good gifts unto your children, how much more shall your Father give good things to them that ask him. All things whatsoever ye would that men should do unto you, even so do ye also unto them. Not every one that saith unto me, Lord . . . but he that doeth the will of my Father. Freely ye have received, freely give. It is more blessed to give than to receive. He that findeth his life shall lose it: and he that loseth his life for my sake shall find it. I thank thee, Father . . . that thou hast hid these things from the wise . . . and revealed them unto babes. Except ye turn and become as little children ye shall in no wise enter into the kingdom of heaven. Forbid them not . . . for to such belongeth the kingdom of heaven. What shall a man be profited if he shall gain the whole world and forfeit his life? It is hard for the rich man to enter into the kingdom of God. Keep yourselves from all covetousness: for a man's life consisteth not in the abundance of the things which he possesseth. The rulers of the Gentiles lord it over them, . . . but whosoever would be great among you shall be your minister; and whosoever would be first among you shall be your servant. Render unto Cæsar the things that are Cæsar's and unto God the things that are God's. Inasmuch as ye did it unto one of the least of these my brethren ye did it unto me. Nevertheless not as I will, but as thou wilt. Father, forgive them, for they know not what they do.

Here is the Christian hope; here its grounds and motives; here rather than in apocalyptic foretellings of the coming of the Son of Man and the near end of the world. Here is an anthology of testimonies to the faith which a world at war to end war most needs, that man is a spiritual being and that his proper work is "to interpret the world according to his higher nature," and to bring the material aspects of the world into subjection to the spirit. Other "oracles and prophecies of loveliness and loving-kindness" in the Bible and in the world's literature have their abiding worth, but no other of "the seers and poets of mankind" reach humanity so widely and none so deeply.

Certain marks and tests of the Christian hope come clearly into view in these characteristic sayings of Jesus. It is a hope not imposed upon the mind by the outward authority of a book or even of Christ himself, but one that appeals to conscience. Our spirit answers to it, and our answer is not only the consent of the mind but the disclosure of character and the choice of the will. It is a hope for which we cannot merely wait, for we are ourselves challenged to bring it to realization. The Christian hope is fundamentally inward, and is always in part already experienced. Paul and John knew the mind of Christ in this striking quality of it better than later generations. The spirit of God is already a love that creates unity and fellowship among men; and it is already the presence and power of divine and eternal life. The Christian hope unites the community and the individual, and contains the clue to the mystery that now obscures our minds. We know that the ruthless sacrifice of individuals for the abstract idol called the State is a denial of Christ's reverence for the human personality. But we know also that the devotion of the soldier's life to the cause of human liberty and right, to the destruction of the idol of nationality and the creation of the ideal brotherhood of man, is in accordance with that giving of life for many which Jesus taught, and is that loss which is the true finding of life. The Christian hope is too inward and too secure to depend on outward success. The doctrine of physical force is judged by physical success, but not the doctrine of love. Yet though superior to outward fortune, the hope of Christ is certain of ultimate vindication, because it is hope in

God. It is a hope according to Christ, and for Christ's coming as the ruling spirit in the life of humanity. But if it is a hope for Christ, if it is Christ's hope for the coming Kingdom of God, it is a hope for radical change, and for the sacrifice of our prejudices and customs, our personal wishes and our material advantage.

The hope for a new world-order which is the most significant spiritual event of our age, requires religion if it is to maintain itself and work powerfully for its own realization. For it is the hope for a purified human nature as well as for a changed human organization. Christianity is the chief source of this hope, and is summoned to prove itself equal to the task of keeping the hope high and giving it inward energy and resource. But it will require boldness of faith and the spirit of sacrifice, a sense of the excellence and worth of spiritual things, and willingness to trust our own souls and the souls of our fellow men, to trust ourselves to the instincts and ways of a Christ-like love, if the Christian hope is to prove able to create a new world.

IV

NON-RESISTANCE: CHRISTIAN OR PAGAN?

BENJAMIN WISNER BACON

ALL forms of peace propaganda are at present justly and properly repressed by the Government as a war measure. This has served in some degree to silence the voice of the pacifist, but manifestly it cannot serve to quiet the disturbed feeling in the minds of many Christians, that to engage in war under any conditions is to come short of the idealism of Jesus. Forcible measures produce the reverse effect, if any.

Non-resistance, under some circumstances and conditions if not under all, is a duty which Jesus undeniably taught. Moreover, his conduct was fully in accord with his principles; otherwise his following could not have maintained their unparalleled loyalty to him. The manifest inconsistency between these non-resistance sayings (taken by themselves) and the method advocated and used by our Government in defence of democracy and righteousness remains ever present. The grave extent of its inroads upon the national morale may be judged by the circulation attained by a typical pacifistic book, whose principal basis of argument is nothing else than these non-resistance sayings, and which if it does not attempt to square them in all cases with the conduct of Jesus, but rather accords to Buddha, Confucius, and Lao-tse the merit of greater consistency, nevertheless owes all its real effect to the fact that its author speaks as a well-known and authorized exponent of Christian teaching, and leaves in his readers' minds the conviction not of the alleged inconsistency, but of an absolute and unqualified doctrine of non-resistance as supported by both the teaching and the conduct of Jesus.

The single year 1915-1916 witnessed the appearance of no less than five successive editions of the book entitled "New Wars for Old," by Rev. John Haynes Holmes, and its propaganda of absolute and unconditional non-resistance was certainly not without effect in the military cantonments, if not among the public at large where its influence is less easy to trace. Recently the Government itself has given public and official warning against this type of pacifistic propaganda; and there is only too much reason to believe that (quite without the intention or knowledge of its authors) those eminent pacifists, the Potsdam conspirators, have made large financial contributions to its success.

"New Wars for Old" may be taken as representative. It is the best example of its type. It seems to be the most effective. At all events, it gives concrete and tangible form to that interpretation of the teaching of Jesus which we regard as misleading and dangerous; it may therefore well form our starting-point toward the attainment of another interpretation, truer at once to historical fact and to the ethical sense of the religious-minded. Recognizing the need for meeting present conditions of the public mind by other than merely repressive measures we may frankly face the question raised in Dr. Holmes' book, whether the doctrine of absolute and unqualified non-resistance, traced by him to more than one revered teacher of pre-Christian paganism, is indeed identical with that of Jesus; or whether, with Israel's Messianic hope, some new factor enters in, to differentiate the Biblical ideal.

Isaiah and Jesus are for this champion of pacifism—and doubtless for others—the two supreme "exemplars of non-resistance," and the eloquence with which his thesis is maintained might well win an assent which would not be granted were account taken of his authority to pronounce upon questions of historical criticism. However, few Americans, competent to form a moral judgment of their own, will hold in light esteem the authority of Isaiah and

Jesus. We therefore accept the exemplars at the risk of seeing our native hue of resolution all sicklied o'er with this pale cast of thought. But is their teaching justly and fairly interpreted? That is the question to which we now address ourselves.

I

"'Resist not evil,' means never resist, never oppose violence." Such is the motto, quoted from Tolstoy, with which our propagandist heads his pages. As he cites no other scholar, critic, or interpreter of the Sermon on the Mount, in support of this declaration of the meaning, the inference is perhaps allowable that the reader is expected to endow Tolstoy with a credit for scientific attainments in the difficult field of historical criticism and interpretation equally great with that which all men gladly accord to his noble disposition and sincere humanity. Whether authority as convincing can be cited for the contention that Buddha and Lao-tse taught the same doctrine of absolute non-resistance we are not competent to say. It seems at least to be beautifully expressed in the saying quoted from Buddha:

> With mercy and forbearance shalt thou disarm every foe. For want of fuel the fire expires: mercy and forbearance bring violence to naught.

What Christian will deny the Christ-likeness of this teaching? What reader of the Old Testament will not hasten to add with Paul from Jewish "wisdom":

> If thine enemy hunger feed him, if he thirst give him drink; for by so doing thou shalt heap coals of fire upon his head.[1]

If, indeed, the duty in question be that of *forbearance*, all great religious teachers, whether of Christian or pre-Christian times, will be at one. "Hymns of hate" are unknown to the ritual of any religion, unless it be the ultra-modern of Prussian militarism. One must go to Nietzsche before attaining to the gospel that it is virtuous to have a giant's strength and use it like a giant.

[1] Rom. 12:20, citing Prov. 25:21-22.

Teachers such as Buddha and Lao-tse may well have added to the well-nigh universal religious tenet of mercy, forgiveness, forbearance, the further doctrine of consistent, unqualified non-resistance. We accept it for the obvious reason that their systems of thought, which are philosophies rather than religions, contain (so far as the present writer is aware) no principle of active, but only of passive obligation. The chief end of man is for them not to achieve, in loyal service to the Creator's ideal, but to abstain and refrain, to put the brakes on life, and to teach others to do the like. According to the author of "New Wars for Old," Buddha and Lao-tse lived up to their gospel of non-resistance. Contrariwise, "The Nazarene had his inconsistent moments like the rest of us," and showed it at this point. Our propagandist is too honest to palter with the quibble of Adin Ballou, who in his "Christian Non-Resistance" argues that Jesus in cleansing the temple may have driven the money-changers from the courtyard, but that there is no evidence that he struck any one of them. With such apologetic special pleading he has no patience, preferring to give the act of Jesus its full weight in the following straightforward words:

What we have here is a well-authenticated violation of the principle of non-resistance—and why not accept it as such? The episode is chiefly remarkable in the life of the Nazarene, not for anything which it teaches in itself, but for its inconsistency with the rest of his career. Never at any other time, so far as we know, did he precipitate riot or himself assault his enemies. But this time he did—this time he failed to live up to the inordinately exacting demands of his own gospel of brotherhood. Nor is the circumstance at all difficult to understand! Jesus came to Jerusalem tired, worn, hunted. He knew that he walked straight into the arms of his enemies, and undoubtedly therefore straight to his own death. Weary, desperate, confused, he came to the temple to pray—and here, right before the altars of his God, were the money-changers—here in the sacred places, the type and symbol of that commercialized religion which he most abhorred, and which he knew was certain in the end to destroy him. What wonder that a mighty flood of anger surged up in his soul, and for the moment overwhelmed him.

In short, the weary Jesus was so irritated by the unexpected (?) sight of the traders, that he threw to the winds not only his principles, but the dictates of the most ordinary prudence, giving his enemies not only their desired opportunity, but provoking the issue at just the point where he himself had been betrayed into the violation of his own teaching. Verily, great is the insight of the modern psychologist. To the observer of the phenomena of petulance an incident like the cleansing of the temple is "easy to understand." The scientific imagination required is easily attained. One acquires it by observing the irritability of tired children. How needless, then, to inform oneself as to the historical conditions which made this great symbolic act of the Galilean prophet full of meaning to every patriot Jew that witnessed it. How needless to raise the question why every one of our four evangelists should report the act and give it the prominence they do. For our evangelists record it reluctantly, minimizing its political significance and its insurrectionary flavor. They naturally disliked to give color of justice to Pilate's judicial murder, and to Jewish denunciations of the new religion as a rebellion against established authority.

Let us then take as our point of departure this admitted "inconsistency." It is not historical interpretation, but the subjective variety sometimes self-designated "psychological" which finds it "easy" to set aside the representation of the oldest and most reliable of our sources, that Jesus was *not* "weary, desperate, confused," and was not in the least taken unawares, when he drove the traders from the temple; but that he planned his *coup de main* with careful deliberation. The evening *before,* says Mark, "he entered the temple and looked round upon all things." Jesus was not unaware of the conditions he would find, for they were an abuse as notorious as hateful to every right-minded Israelite. This even the Talmud attests. He was not a hunted fugitive seeking asylum at the altar. On the contrary, for weeks past he had set his face steadfastly to go to Jerusalem and there lift up the standard of the Son of David. The initiative was his. He had planned a new campaign for his ideal, the Kingdom of God, a campaign no longer of mere teaching but of action, and he was now carrying it to the very seat of hostile power. Long since, probably before he left Galilee, he had planned this very act, a challenge to the corrupt priestly control of his Father's house, an act as full of meaning and as deliberate as Luther's nailing of his theses to the church doors of Wittenberg.

And when the blow had been struck Jesus stood courageously by it. He met the inevitable demand of the hierocracy, "By what authority doest thou these things?" with a counter demand. Whence had the Baptist authority to inaugurate his prophetic reform, making ready for Jehovah a purified people prepared for his coming? The Sanhedrin evaded this counter demand, and answered only (as Jesus had foreseen they would) by secret denunciation of him to Pilate. But Pilate understood the case. We have the Roman governor's official interpretation of its significance in a certain superscription written aloft in Hebrew and Greek and Latin on the gibbet of an insurrectionist. This, too, Jesus seems to have foreseen.

All this was not a mere "episode." It was the culminating effort and crisis of Jesus' career, and richly rewards a just understanding. We are told that it was "inconsistent with the rest of Jesus' career." His mission, we infer, was to be a rabbi. His attempt at active leadership in achieving the Kingdom he preached was an unfortunate aberration. He should not have tried to be "the Christ," and thereby incurred a needless martyrdom. The cross is still a stumblingblock.

Strange that the evangelists who omit so much, who would have so strong a motive for omitting this particular "inconsistency" no less for their Master's good name than for the safety of the Church, should one and all record it. The disposition to minimize everything savoring of political action on Jesus' part is very marked in all our evangelists, for obvious reasons. To the evidences of this belong, for example, Mark's denial, and the fourth evangelist's explanation, of the saying about destroying the temple, together with the latter's description of the whip "of small cords" as Jesus' only weapon in the purging of the temple.[2] Are we then to admit the "inconsistency"—not casual and incidental, as conceived in this pacifistic interpretation, but deliberate and flagrant? Or may we perhaps now raise the question whether the "inconsistency" is not rather chargeable to the interpreter's account?

The interpretation with which we are dealing makes the teaching of Jesus regarding the use of force identical with the non-resistance doctrine of Buddha and Lao-tse. On the other hand, it very justly relates it to that of the great prophet of the Davidic kingdom of righteousness and peace, Isaiah, the son of Amoz. From the point of view of the historical critic the relation of Jesus' teaching to that of Isaiah is absolutely sound. But the effect of this relation is fatal to its identification with the non-resistance doctrine of Buddha and Lao-tse.

Apart from the circumstances which for the time being made non-resistance, or rather mere passive resistance, the policy of true statesmanship alike against Assyrian and against Roman domination, Isaiah and Jesus stood together upon the most fundamental point of all, unqualified, unlimited loyalty to the God of Righteousness and to his sovereignty upon earth. Their pacifism differs from that of Lao-tse and of Buddha in the important respect of having a pronounced theistic basis. Buddha and Lao-tse can preach consistently a doctrine of absolute non-resistance because their systems are destitute of the social ideal of Israel's religion, and indeed ignore the very existence of a "Power not ourselves

[2] See below as to the fourth evangelist's explanation of Jesus' claim to be the Davidic Shepherd of Israel only in the sense of uniting the scattered flock of God.

that makes for Righteousness." Contrariwise with the great prophets of the Kingdom of God. Whether of the Christian or pre-Christian dispensation, so far as they advocate non-resistance it cannot be unlimited, *because their religious aim is not merely individual but social.*

The non-resistance of Isaiah and of Jesus is not self-centered but God-centered. It is bound to consider what is expedient for others, for the weak and dependent, as well as for the individual, and for the present time. It seeks the welfare of the world and of generations to come. It is always subsidiary to the paramount interest of the Kingdom of God.

Just because it regards non-resistance not as an end in itself but only as one of the divinest means to an end, Biblical pacifism can hold before men's eyes the moving figure of the martyred Servant, dumb as the lamb in the shearer's hands, while it can in the same breath commend the men of violence that take the Kingdom of Heaven by force. Christian or pre-Christian, it rests upon the foundation of utter, absolute loyalty to a world-wide Republic of God, a cosmic sovereignty of righteousness, and having this social aim for its religious ideal it can and does nourish to the highest pitch of devotion the heroic virtues of patriotism, of service and of sacrifice. The summons to the standard (not men's but God's) is ever the same. The weapon may be the sword or the cross, as the times require. Under mere self-centered philosophies such as those of Buddha and Lao-tse the contrary is true. Notoriously, where these control patriotism and all its heroic virtues tend to dwindle, approaching often the verge of extinction.

The pacifism (not non-resistance) of Isaiah hardly requires elucidation. Two or three very familiar quotations will suffice. There is, for example, the prophet's vision of a universal peace based on international law. This vision of the world's willing acceptance of the sovereignty of Jehovah's justice Isaiah shares with his contemporary, Micah, both prophets seeming to choose it as a text from some forgotten earlier pacifist.

It shall come to pass in the latter days
That the mountain of Jehovah's house shall be
stablished at the head of mountains,
And shall be exalted above the hills,
And all nations shall flow unto it.

And many peoples shall go and say, Come, let us
go up to the mountain of Jehovah,
To the house of the God of Jacob,
And he will teach us of his ways, and we will walk
in his paths.
For out of Zion shall go forth law, and the word of
Jehovah from Jerusalem.

And he shall judge between the nations, and will
be arbiter for many peoples;
And they shall beat their swords into plow-shares,
and their spears into pruning-hooks.
Nation shall not lift up sword against nation,
Neither shall they learn war any more.

Manifestly the ideal of an international tribunal as the basis of a League of Peace is not so novel as some modern statesmanship seems to conceive.

But the consistent, thoroughgoing advocate of non-resistance rejects even the coercion of magisterial and police constraint. To Russian idealism restraint of the individual as well as the national criminal is tainted with the same poison of violence. Since Isaiah is the exemplar of non-resistance he should be permitted again to speak for himself. His words seem to have a singular applicability to the land which is now testing to the limit the theory of Proudhon, the individualist of individualists, the gospel of anarchism:

For behold the Lord, Jehovah of Hosts, doth take away from
Jerusalem and from Judah stay and staff,
The whole stay of bread and the whole stay of water,
The mighty man, and the man of war;

The judge and the prophet, the diviner and the elder;
The captain of fifty and the honorable man and the counsellor . . .
And I will give children to be their princes,
And with childishness shall they rule over them,
And the people shall be oppressed every one by another, and every one by his neighbor:
The child shall be arrogant against the old man, and the base against the honorable.

But Isaiah, too, expects deliverance from these miseries of foreign servitude and domestic anarchy. He looks for the dawn of a just and lasting peace; only the means of its attainment seem strange for an "exemplar of non-resistance."

The people that walked in darkness have seen a great light;
They that dwelt in the land of the shadow of death, upon them hath the light shined.
Thou hast multiplied the nation and increased their joy,
They joy before thee according to the rejoicing at harvest-time,
As men rejoice when they divide the spoil.
For the yoke of (Israel's) burden, and the rod laid to his shoulder,
The staff of his oppressor, thou hast broken as in the day of Midian.

For all the armor of the armed man in the tumult
And the garments rolled in blood shall be for burning, for fuel of fire.
For unto us a child is born, unto us a son is given,
And the government shall be upon his shoulder:
And his name shall be called: Wonderful-counsellor;
The-Mighty-God-the-Everlasting (my)-Father;
The Prince of Peace.

Of the increase of his government and of peace there shall be no end.
Upon the throne of David and upon his kingdom,
To establish it, and to uphold it with justice and with righteousness from henceforth even forever.
The zeal of Jehovah of Hosts will perform this.

Even with the devout restraint of the closing line it must be admitted that these verses have a somewhat martial ring.

Doubtless the pacifist will emphasize the line, "The zeal of Jehovah of Hosts will perform this," taking here the view of the Pharisees, who in contrast with the fanatical nationalism of the Zealots opposed the aggressive militarism of the later Maccabees with a doctrine of quietism. Their cry was, "Leave all to God." Against the Zealot they appealed to the proverb: "They that take the sword shall perish by the sword," from which the inference is plain that if the aim be never to lose one's life one should never take weapons. But perhaps Isaiah the "non-resistant" is entitled to one more chance to prove himself not a Pharisee, even when he expects "the zeal of Jehovah of Hosts" to win the victory of peace. Fortunately he tells us *how* he expects the zeal of Jehovah to operate, in the doom he pronounces upon "drunkard" Samaria, the city whose luxuriant mountain-top was crowned with mingled towers and olive groves, like the fading wreaths upon the heads of drunken revellers. In contrast to Samaria's fate Isaiah has this promise for the temple-crowned hill of Zion, shadowed under its altar smoke:

> In that day will Jehovah of Hosts become a crown of glory
> And a diadem of beauty unto the residue of his people,
> *A spirit of justice to him that sitteth in judgment,*
> *And a spirit of strength to them that turn back the battle at the gate.*[3]

II

It should hardly be necessary to explain that Jesus in deliberately giving up the career of purely non-political preacher, teacher, and healer, to assume the career of *Christ* and Son of David, fully

[3] The citations are all from the unquestioned writings of the First Isaiah, Isa. 2:2-4; 3:1-5; 9:2-7 and 28:1-6. The rendering is made independently from the Hebrew.

conscious as he was of all the dangers it implied, was neither ignorant of the Isaian ideal, nor out of sympathy with it. When he rode into Jerusalem accepting the acclamation: "Blessed be the kingdom that cometh, the kingdom of our father David," he was not betraying the national hope; he was lifting it toward ultimate realization at the cost of Calvary.

It is true that he avoided suicidal collision with Roman authority on the one side, as prudently as he forestalled the sweeping off of his following into the insane fanaticism of the Zealot nationalists on the other. The prophet's method of a symbolic purifying of the temple was exactly suited to this purpose. In the temple Roman authority explicitly renounced control. The policing of this combined fortress, sanctuary, and treasure house was left, even to the power of life and death, in the hands of the Sadducean hierocracy. It was administered by a numerous and efficient Levite police commanded by a "captain of the temple." On the other hand, Sadducean control was notoriously and infamously corrupt. The abuses by which (with their connivance) money was extorted from the worshippers made it so hateful that a worthy reformer might be sure of popular support strong enough to cow "the hissing brood of Annas" into an interval of "fear of the people." And the reform might even be accomplished without unchaining the red fool-fury of the Zealot mob, if it was seen to be the work of a prophet, by authority "from heaven" and not "of men," consistent, even if regarded as a messianic act, with the course of one who had come "meek and lowly and having salvation, riding upon an ass, and on a colt the foal of an ass."

It is of vital importance to a historical appreciation of Jesus' sense of his mission to realize fully and adequately what he meant by this one public overt act of his career; for by it he signalized to all Israel assembled at the Passover his purpose to achieve a national deliverance such as the feast commemorated. From it every loyal Israelite might infer that the hope of "the kingdom of David" was now about to be realized. Jesus thus entered deliberately upon the stormy and dangerous seas of messianistic agitation, as a claimant to leadership in the achievement of the national hope.

To herald such a reform as Jesus proposed, reviving the national ideal, the purification of the temple was a symbolic act worthy of the greatest of prophets. It was exactly fitted to raise and define the issues at stake. It would convey just the right impression to the multitude, whose attention could be reached by this time-honored method, and by this method alone. It was also free from the worst dangers of messianistic agitation. It would avoid on the one hand the Scylla of needless collision with Roman authority, and on the other the Charybdis of Zealot turbulence. The calm and fearless "authority from heaven" with which it was effected overawed resistance, so that even while asserted *by force* it attained its result with the shedding of no other blood than the Messenger's own.

To show the exact meaning to contemporary Jewish minds of this act of the Prophet of Nazareth we must recall not merely the Isaian ideal of the "Davidic" reign as a universal kingdom of righteousness and peace based on divine law going forth from Zion, but also the later apocalyptic hopes. We must remember that all expectation in Jesus' time was focussed on the prophecies of Malachi, which made the purified temple the scene of Jehovah's visitation of his people, after they should have been brought to a "great repentance" by the coming of Elias. A rabbinic parable of the period will give us the point of view. It is an answer to the reproach so bitterly resented by Isaiah, "Israel is a wife forsaken," and is based on Malachi 1:6-14, and 3:1-12 interpreting the designation "Tent of Witness" applied to the tabernacle in Exodus 38:21:

A king was angry with his wife and forsook her. The neighbors declared, "He will not return" (cf. Isa. 49:14). Then the king sent word to her (Mal. 1:10 ff): "Cleanse my palace, and on such and such a day I will return to thee." He came and was reconciled to her.

Therefore is the sanctuary called the Tent of "Witness"—a witness to the Gentiles that God is no longer wroth.[4]

Jesus' act was the assertion of authority "from heaven" to make Jehovah's will supreme upon earth, beginning at his own sanctuary. It was effected by direct appeal to the conscience of the masses, which to the extent of their understanding responded overwhelmingly. Jesus did not expect his act to be more than "a witness to the peoples." But on the other hand, for the time being at least, he sacrificed no life save his own. One close parallel could be cited from modern times if the demonstration could be freed from its unfortunate association with really fanatical revolt and real intention to provoke a servile insurrection. In keeping his demonstration in the temple free from entangling alliance with Zealot nationalism, Jesus showed a moderation and foresight which were unfortunately lacking to the demonstration of John Brown at Harpers Ferry; otherwise the two have many points of affinity. It was while the governor of Virginia was still hesitating to sign the death warrant of the champion of negro emancipation, long before his martyr spirit marched on before great armies of liberation, that Ralph Waldo Emerson, once himself a non-resistant pacifist, wrote in his journal:

If John Brown shall suffer, he will make the gallows glorious like the cross.

III

THAT Jesus intended to raise the standard of David by his public act at the Passover is certain. His pacifism was of the type of Micah's and Isaiah's. That he meant the act to convey a religious sense differentiating it from the merely political ideal of the Zealots is also certain. His doctrine of reliance on spiritual methods in the pursuit of the God-given aim exalts forbearance *as a means* in terms not less noble than the foremost champions of non-resistance. We may question whether he actually counted

[4] Mal. 3:1-4; 4:1-6.

upon his own only too probable fate of crucifixion at Roman hands as destined to serve the precise end which it actually has subserved in human history. Those who see it with the wisdom of retrospect know that it has furnished to all devotees of Israel's ideal of the Kingdom of God, in all races, unto all successive generations, a rallying point and a symbol of final victory. But Jesus was looking forward with the eye of faith, not backward with the eye of knowledge. He believed that even through death God would give victory to those who sacrificed life and all to his kingdom's cause, and that it would be given ere their generation had passed into oblivion. How much further than this his prophetic insight into the ways of God with men extended is a question which will be variously answered in accordance with varying views of his personality. It need be no matter of surprise, however, to any discerning mind, that the fourth evangelist should also look backward at the significance of the cross, interpreting it in the light of its actual results. The fourth evangelist is the successor of Paul at Ephesus. Like Paul he naturally emphasizes its effect in "reconciliation," a twofold atonement, "breaking down the enmity" between man and God, and also that between man and man; and the great barrier of Paul's experience was that erected by the Mosaic law between Jew and Gentile. By the cross, says Paul to the Ephesians, Christ who is "our peace"[5]

> made both one, and brake down the middle wall of partition, having abolished in his flesh the enmity; even the law of commandments contained in ordinances, that he might create in himself of the twain one new man, so making peace; and might reconcile them both in one body unto God through the cross, having slain the enmity thereby.

No wonder Paul thinks of God as "the God of peace," the gospel as "the gospel of peace" and Christ as "our peace" proclaimed to the nations near and far.

That is the pacifism of Christianity. No wonder Paul's great successor at Ephesus compares this healing and reconciling cross

[5] Paul is elaborating Isa. 57:19.

to the token of forgiveness and faith which Moses lifted up in the wilderness, and repeatedly presents as its divinely appointed aim the "gathering into one the children of God that are scattered abroad" (John 11:51-52).

The fourth evangelist devotes the closing section of his story of the public ministry to this great question, Why Jesus came forward as the Christ? The scene he chooses is Jerusalem at the Feast of Dedication, that festival which commemorated the death and resurrection of the Maccabean martyrs who had given their lives for the national ideal. The story begins with the Jews' demand of Jesus that he "tell them plainly" whether he is the Christ. It ends with the mystical utterance of the high priest:

> that Jesus should die for the nation, and not for that nation only, but that he might gather together into one the children of God which are scattered abroad.

To show what alternative lay before him we are told of a delegation of Greeks who wait upon Jesus, apparently to invite him to "go to the Gentiles and teach them," but who receive as their answer, after a momentary soul-conflict paralleling the scene of Gethsemane, that Jesus "must be lifted up," and thus through his martyr death "will draw all men unto him." The central scene of the raising of Lazarus is of course directed to the resurrection theme appropriate to this feast, the theme of the Christ who as Messenger of God brings life and immortality to light. But the whole section rests back on an opening parable, that of the Good Shepherd who lays down his life for the sheep (John 10:11-18). Our concern is with this parable; for it is not an invention of the fourth evangelist, but an authentic comparison of Jesus attested by the preceding evangelists,[6] and merely developed in the later interpretative gospel along the lines of the original prophecy,[7] and with special reference to the cross as a token of

[6] Mk. 6:34; 14:27 and parallels.

[7] Ezek. 34.

unity in estranged and warring humanity evoked by loyalty to a common higher ideal.

In the parable of the Good Shepherd, as elsewhere, the fourth evangelist shows that his view of the tragedy of Calvary is determined by its actual result. The function of the Shepherd is to gather a flock now scattered, and which includes "other sheep that are not of this fold." The aim is "that there may be one flock; one Shepherd," an aim suggested by Paul. But primarily the parable is simply an adaptation of Ezekiel's famous indictment of the hireling shepherds of Israel, who had first exploited Jehovah's flock, and then abandoned it to the ravening of wild beasts. Because of this, the prophet declares, Jehovah himself will seek out the scattered and bleeding remnant and will set up over them a worthy shepherd, the son of David.

The special application made by the fourth evangelist is to the gathering of a flock already scattered, bleeding, and torn of beasts, because of the faithlessness of hireling shepherds. Such was in truth the task imposed by the conditions of the time. Such was in the experience of Paul and his generation the actual effect of the cross. But primarily and in Jesus' mind it was simply the token of the last supreme measure of devotion which he, and all who would follow him, must be prepared to pay in loyalty to the Kingdom of God. Its comparison is purely and simply a contrast between two types of leadership. On the one side is he who lays down his life in defence of the helpless, be it in conflict, as when David the shepherd lad with sling and stone rescued his sheep "out of the paw of the lion and the bear," or be it in search for the lost lamb upon the mountainside. On the other side is he who "when he seeth the wolf coming leaveth the sheep and fleeth." The special need of the time, that which appealed to Jesus as the supreme need of those to whom he was sent, was his people's need of a standard and leadership, rescue of the scattered and lost.

When he saw the multitude he had compassion on them because they were distressed and scattered as sheep that have no shepherd.

He gave them the needed rallying point, a sign in which afterward they should conquer. He also gave them the needed leadership. The former was the need of the first age of the Church. The second need is ours; for defence of the flock is as much a shepherd's task as seeking out the lost. They who abandon it in the face of wolfish attack need expect no approval from the Son of David.

IV

THERE is a certain magnificence of logical consistency in the non-resistance doctrine of the pacifist who chooses the Empire of China (!) as the example of its perfect work in the field of international relations.[8] With the blessed example of the Celestial Kingdom before us we are asked:

> What did it avail Belgium to marshal her armies and hold her forts against the irresistible advance of the German legions?[9]

The question has an extraordinary resemblance to that addressed by the Kaiser to King Albert in *Punch's* famous cartoon: "Don't you see that Belgium has lost everything?" And Albert's answer is taken from Christ's own lips: "She has not lost her soul." The Celestial Empire on the other hand seems to this champion of the pacifism of Lao-tse to have practically realized the blessings of the Kingdom of Heaven. Peacefully non-resistant under the corrupt domination of its Manchu conquerors it had attained the climax of earthly felicity. It had a name to live, and was dead.

> The Chinese and the Quakers, each in their own way, are finished products. What they are is all they ever can be. Which means from the standpoint of national idealism, that non-resistance is the "saving element."[10]

This eulogy of China, however, was written before the new Republic of China, stirring the long dormant instincts of Chinese

8 "New Wars for Old," pp. 252-258.

9 *Ibid.* p. 223.

10 *Ibid.* p. 258.

patriotism, had roused to new hopes and visions of world achievement the body that had become as one dead, insomuch that the more part said, He is dead. But non-resistant pacifism is ever rich in paradox. Today China herself, so long inert, blessed for so many centuries with all the felicity of submission, has thrown off the Manchu yoke of domination. And in the first surge of new-found strength she declares war against Attila and his Huns, and in the declaration itself avows that she is "fighting to establish peace." To such inconsistency does non-resistance seem fated as soon as life triumphs over death, as soon as the Christian gospel of a world kingdom of righteousness and peace triumphs over Buddha's pessimistic obliteration of desire and hope together in the gray *nirvana* of extinction. "Eternal life" through death-defying loyalty to a divine ideal begins at last to seem preferable, even in China, to mere indefinite "survival."

Not Quakerdom itself seems able to maintain consistency with its non-resistant ideals. Alas,

> they were abandoned by those who could not and would not see the connection between these principles and the uninterrupted peace which had long blessed the Pennsylvania colony.

Becoming itself directly responsible for the order and security hitherto guaranteed by the sovereign British power the Quaker commonwealth followed the example of its neighbor states and girt on the sword.[11] For this, doubtless, we may hold the influx of alien immigrants more responsible than the genuine followers of Fox and Penn. But it must at least be admitted that Quaker leaven showed little power to work, so far as the doctrine and policy of non-resistance are concerned.

Inconsistencies such as these on the part of the greatest modern exemplars of non-resistance are saddening to its champions, but there remains ever a more ethereal realm, where philosophy can build without fear of the stern realities of life, the limbo of utopias.

11 "New Wars for Old," p. 241.

V

Jesus, too, they tell us, though greatest of all non-resistants, was also "inconsistent." Was he, then, inconsistent with himself? Or was his pacifism the active pacifism of those who give their lives for just and lasting peace, the peace that is real and not mere devastation, not destruction and tyranny miscalled *Kultur;* not might triumphant over right and unashamed; but a peace that endures because justice and right have been enthroned?

Jesus closed his public teaching with the doctrine that all religion, all duty to God and man, is summed up in the two commandments: Unreserved, unqualified, unfaltering devotion to the One God of Righteousness and Truth; unselfish devotion to the common weal of man. One who in obedience to this law of love took up the succession of Moses, David and the prophets, raising the standard of God's real sovereignty on earth, and paying to it the last full measure of his own devotion, has not deserved the accusation of inconsistency. Jesus was sublimely consistent. That interpretation of his words which refuses the witness of his heroic deeds to their true meaning is guilty of the inconsistency.

It is true, as Tolstoy finely says, that Jesus' noble depiction in the Sermon on the Mount of the forbearance of God as the standard of the higher righteousness means that we should "never do anything *contrary to the law of love.*" But by what right does the great Russian pacifist (or any other who claims for his theory the authority of Jesus) omit from that law of love its "first and great commandment"? How can we ignore the demand of supreme and unqualified devotion to the God of Righteousness, whose kingdom of righteous peace Jesus gave his life to establish, and limit our obedience to acquiescence in the demands of men, be they righteous or the reverse? The second commandment of the Law of Love is dependent on the first, and in separation from it will assuredly be misconstrued. Equal love of neighbor can be no requirement of *religion,* save as it depends on the prior obligation of supreme devotion to a common Father, whose forbearing, forgiving love extends equally to all. Imitation of that Father's goodness and forbearance, overcoming the evil of the world with good, is the one teaching, the comprehensive, unifying principle, of the Sermon on the Mount. But the God whose goodness this great discourse sets up as the standard of the righteousness of all "sons and daughters of the Highest" is not a *non-resistant* God. It is the just and merciful God depicted in those Scriptures wherein Jesus read his beneficent will and purpose for the world.

It is not enough for the Christian merely "to do nothing contrary to the law of love"; he must actively toil and suffer in its service, fighting to the death. His personal enemy he may and must forgive. Enemies have thus been won to the kingdom. The enemy of the weak and defenceless brother he must resist. The enemy of God's kingdom he must fight to the death. It is true that this foe of God is no human or visible foe. Our wrestling is not against flesh and blood; it is against the principalities and powers of darkness in the heavenly places. But we do not beat the air. This power of darkness finds incarnation in human form at least as readily as the Power of light. He fights with real and concrete weapons, and this reality is the ultimate test. For the foe who thus incarnates the evil power the Christian has no hatred as brother-man; only as agent of the evil power. The hatred ceases when the man renounces the evil allegiance. Hence the paradox of love that may necessitate a blow. Self-deception is here all too easy, but absolutely selfless devotion may be trusted even here not to substitute its own cause for God's.

The very paragraph from which the non-resistants draw their doctrine has this conclusion:

> Wherefore seek ye *first* the kingdom of God and his righteousness, and all these (outward blessings) shall be added unto you.

It is because Jesus sought *first* the kingdom, which means righteousness, peace and good will among men, sovereignty of right over might, overthrow of the powers of darkness which claim as their own the kingdoms of the world and the glory of them, that he could teach as the best means to its attainment forbearance and loving-kindness to the limit. For a limit there is—the *divine* limit of the welfare of all. Loyalty to this ideal led Jesus to crown his sublime teaching with action sublimer still. When the scenes of his earlier ministry were closed, he left the quiet paths of teacher and healer in Galilee to tread the martyr's road, and to set up in his own cross an ensign to rally the scattered and bleeding flock of God. Because he sought "first the kingdom of God" Jesus held back his disciples from the bloody and disastrous path of Zealot fanaticism, and bade Peter return his futile sword to its sheath. For the same reason and no other he depicted to his disciples the Good Shepherd laying down his life in defence of the flock, and poured scorn upon the hireling who "when he seeth the wolf coming, leaveth the sheep and fleeth." It is for the same reason and no other that he also warned them of days to come when it should be the duty of the disciple unprovided with a sword to "sell his garment and buy one," days when only he that endured unto the end, fighting to the death against the powers of darkness, should be saved.

Jesus teaches *unlimited* non-resistance where only personal and selfish interests are at stake; but resistance unto blood for the sake of the Kingdom of God and his righteousness. In this he *is* inconsistent with non-resistant pacifism that can see no difference between this doctrine and that of Buddha or Lao-tse. Jesus even reverses that Bolshevist pacifism that to save its own skin throws to the Turkish-Teuton wolves the bleeding remnant of the earliest historic flock of Christ. He approves rather shepherds that give their lives fighting in defence of their helpless charge. He *is* inconsistent with the theories and philosophies of non-resistance; but he is consistent, sublimely consistent, with his own gospel of the sovereignty of God.

The rule of truly Christian pacifism is not hard to understand when we approach it from the standpoint of those who after the precept and example of Jesus seek *first* the Kingdom of God. Men of this type are ready like "all the saints who nobly fought of old" to lose their lives in this high cause, that they may save them unto life eternal. For individuals and for nations the rule is the same: "In thine own cause strike never, not even in self-defence; in God's cause strike when he bids thee strike and cease not, come victory or death." There is, no doubt, an easy self-delusion, prone to identify its own cause with God's. But against this blasphemous egotism human history henceforth will ever set up the abhorrent warning of a certain imperial attitudinizer whom we do not need to name. There is a time for forbearance, patience, longsuffering, up to the limit of the forbearance of that God who seeks only the good of all, and who seeks it in wisdom and justice as well as in forbearance. The time is *up to that limit*, and not beyond it. If the enemy can be won, win him. Turn the other cheek, surrender tunic along with cloak. But forbearance is not meant to play into the hands of the evil power. There is also a time when it only gluts the ravenous maw of inhuman, soulless tyranny, a time when incarnate evil sits in the very temple of God, setting itself forth as God, a time when the law of violence is openly avowed and exalted above the law of mercy and right, a time of the beast and the false prophet, threatening to turn civilization back again to the age of Lamech and Tubal-cain. That is a time to remember also the commandment, "Let him that hath no sword sell his cloak and buy one," and the promise: "He that overcometh, I will give to him to sit down with me on my throne, as I also overcame, and sat down with my Father on his throne."

V

THE MINISTRY AND THE WAR

HENRY HALLAM TWEEDY

When the greatest crime in all history was perpetrated and the world-war began, it was natural and necessary that the ministry of all lands should buckle on the Christian armor and take its place in the fighting ranks. Thousands volunteered as chaplains and Y. M. C. A. workers. Thousands more—two thousand at one time in Canada alone—equally eager to don the khaki and endure their share of the hardships, waited impatiently until a door could be opened for them to go. In the training camps and in the trenches, in hut and in hospital, these men found new parishes and pulpits, ministering in a multitude of ways, and finding opportunities for Christ-like service in the soldier's every need. They did more than preach sermons, hold Bible classes, and act as spiritual comforters and advisers. To them, as to Donald Hankey's "beloved captain," no task was too petty or too menial, no lowly service beneath them, if it lightened the burdens or added to the comfort and efficiency of the fighters. At all times and everywhere, in all ways and by all means, they strove to represent the Master, who cared for bodies as well as for souls, for the resting times and food and tired feet as well as for the thoughts and motives and ambitions of his disciples. They were the ambassadors of the Prince of Peace and the army's public friends.

All this was only what might have been expected. The arresting fact was to find these prophets of peace, with comparatively few exceptions, proclaiming the righteousness of our participation in the war. In 1915 when the *Continent*, of Chicago, sent out a questionnaire among the Presbyterian ministers of the country, an overwhelming majority declared themselves in favor of preparedness. A vote in Brooklyn, embracing ministers in something like twenty denominations, showed one hundred and fifty-one in favor of preparedness, while six qualified their approval and only fourteen were opposed. These are indications of the trend of thought among the ministers of America; and though they may not give direct and unimpeachable evidence of how these men would have viewed the entrance of the United States into the European *débâcle*, it would seem to be a legitimate inference that their attitude would be the same. When a nation, patient and forbearing until her enemies scoffed and her friends grieved, found herself compelled to defend her unquestioned rights against lawless and brutal pirates, minds which approved of preparedness for war would naturally, almost inevitably, approve of war. Nor was it our rights only. We entered the struggle not through pride or greed or hatred, but as the champion of international law, righteousness, liberty, democracy, and a world peace that shall be abiding and just for all.

To the few pacifists among the clergy all this seems quite unnecessary. Why should not America walk in the footsteps of Jesus, set her face steadfastly toward her Jerusalem, and for the world's salvation suffer Germany and Austria and Turkey to drive the spikes through her hands? Why not permit the Central Powers to seize and possess our country, even though they dealt with those of us, who could not and would not submit to the ethics of Nietzsche and the diplomacy of Bernhardi and the rule of von Hindenburg, as they treated the fathers and mothers and little children of Armenia and Belgium and Poland? "Resist not evil!" The cure of Christ's time is the cure of our time! The age of Judas and of Pilate, of the scribes and brutal Roman soldiers, has never passed.

This is not the place to attempt to settle the dispute between the champions of peace at any price and those of a war which, rightly or wrongly, they regard as righteous and unavoidable. It certainly will never be decided by calling all pacifists cowards and slackers, and all defenders of the course pursued by President Wilson, the son of a clergyman, exponents of Prussian militarism. The plain fact is that there is no path open to us which presents no moral difficulties. It is not a choice between absolute right and absolute wrong, but between the preponderance of right and the preponderance of wrong. As some one has phrased it, "War is a moral enterprise, if it redeems a state from a condition worse than war"; and that—so it seemed to thousands of ethical and religious teachers—was the situation in America. To have watched the violation of Belgium, the massacre of Armenia, the destruction of England, France and Italy, the absorption of Russia, and ultimately the forging of the chains of our own servitude, without striking a blow to protect the world against the unspeakable barbarism of a megalomaniac would have been ethical madness. Granting the culprit's sanity, it would have been a kind of religious paranoia not to bring the international butcher and brigand to terms. The man who stands by, while a thug robs his neighbor's house and murders the wife and children, practically coöperates with the criminal. If he is a saint, he is a saintly Raffles. Though he never strike a blow, he bears the mark of Cain. Leaders like the Rev. Charles A. Eaton, D.D., of the Madison Avenue Baptist Church in New York City, have ventured to characterize our participation in the struggle as "our Christian duty." Many even of our Quakers vigorously champion it. Mr. John L. Carver, the head of the Friends' School in New York and Brooklyn, writes: "First and last, let us have no compromise or suggestion of compromise as to the justice of the American cause—no admixture of false pacifism in relation to one of the few absolutely just and unavoidable wars that the world has ever seen, unmarred by fanaticism, mistaken hatred, or lust of gain. Let us permit no confusion of ideas between old time wars of aggression or revenge, and this present war of unselfish sacrifice to save humanity from the reign of the beast." With this it is safe to say the great majority of Christians, lay and clerical, heartily agree. War is always bad; but there are situations when to decline to give battle, permitting the foe to work his immoral will, is not only still more terrible in its cost but more awful in its moral degradation. To kill is always an evil; but it is less of an evil, both for society and for the evil doer, than to permit a band of deluded assassins to run amuck in the ranks of civilization and to practice their marksmanship on the gentlest of women and the noblest of men. Almost to a man the leaders of thought in the allied countries, with unwilling minds and breaking hearts, have reached this decision. Rightly or wrongly, it is the answer which has come to their agonized petition, "Lord, what wilt thou have me to do?"

But there is a still more striking fact. Not only are our ministers like Sir George Adam Smith in khaki and Dr. Henry Van Dyke in the uniform of the navy, toiling as spiritual specialists for our soldiers and sailors. Not only are teachers like Principal Forsyth and ex-President Taft proclaiming our moral duty and legal right to participate in the greatest and most terrible of wars. After careful deliberation an ever-increasing number of ministers, especially among those of draft age, both in the pastorate and in the seminary, have given up their distinctive work, donned the uniform of the soldier, and sailed for the trenches of France. To some minds this seems incredible folly, a species of ministerial madness. War is so tigerish in its ruthlessness, so demoniacal in its treatment of ethical principles, so un-Christian in matter and in method, that it appears impossible to characterize any participation as righteous. It is, no doubt, the minister's duty to play the rôle of Good Samaritan when, with nations as his victims, the modern Hun repeats the parable. But can he still bear the title of minister if he joins the police force and attempts, even at the cost of killing the robbers, to clean up the Jericho road?

The answer of these men has been an enthusiastic affirmative.

To them their clerical exemption was something more than what Dean Shailer Mathews called it, "an insult or a challenge." No doubt there were good reasons why certain trained specialists, and themselves among them, should be set to work with tools other than bayonets. The physician, the engineer, the munitions expert, the ship-builder and the chaplain will all have their part in the triumph. Mr. Hoover, Mr. Schwab and the Archbishop of York will do more in their present positions than they could behind a machine gun or in an aeroplane. They, and millions of men and women in lowly stations, can fight at home for peace and for freedom; and when the burden is heaviest and the strain almost unendurable, call cheerily, as Harry Lauder did to the Scotch Highlander: "No, man, I'm no tired! If you can die fighting for me, I can die working for you!"

But this patent plea did not satisfy some militant ministers. Their religion as well as their patriotism carried them beyond Dean Mathews' interpretation of the phrase. Grant that their exemption is an insult if it "implies that ministers are not as ready to serve their country as any other citizens, that they are slackers, or that they are so effeminate that they would not make good soldiers; that if they go about their work with no increase of labor or of sacrifice, making an excuse out of their holy calling, they accept their exemption as an insult to their calling." Grant that, if this is not true, it comes to them as a great challenge to do and to dare as much in their spiritual work as the soldier does in his, toiling to the limit of costly sacrifice, possibly to overwork and to death. They are quite ready to burn out, and that quickly, when the age demands the heat and light of their lives. But there was still in their hearts a service unexpressed, an intense desire ungratified. One hears the call in the following letter from a minister, who is now a lieutenant with a Canadian regiment in France:

"I expect to go to the front in Europe in the near future," he wrote to the editor of the *Outlook*. "For six years I was a Presbyterian minister, although a Canadian, in the Presbyterian Church of the United States. When the cause of liberty and the ideals of democracy were at stake, I could not withstand the 'call'—not so much of my country as of civilization—any longer. I resigned my charge and came to Nova Scotia, my boyhood home. It seems strange, but true nevertheless, that today I am a happy man. I hate war and know something about it—I served through the South African War and saw its results—but there are things worse than war. I am going, as I find many of my comrades going, not because we hate the German people, but because we believe that Prussian militarism would be an intolerable system for the world to live under."

"Is this a psychological and moral paradox?" comments the editor. "We think not. Every man who really grasps the meaning of the words righteousness, justice and peace, and their true relations, will understand the state of mind of this Canadian clergyman." It is the decision of one who loves and honors the calling of the ministry, and yet feels that in this crisis there is a place where he, whatever may be true of his fellows, is more greatly needed. It is the confession of faith on the part of a Christian who knows war and hates it, and yet is happy to make it because he loves peace, and believes, rightly or wrongly, that if the world is to possess it in our time, it must be won with the sword. It is the deed of a brother of all men who declines to be limited by his cloth, who cannot preach to the soldier without drinking the soldier's cup and being baptized with his baptism of mud and of blood. It is the spirit of a true Christian preacher, who cannot urge Christian laymen to "go over the top" unless at least some Christian ministers go with them. It is the jubilant response to the call of the heroic, the comradeship which knows no secular and no sacred, and which covets the most intimate fellowship in the life and sufferings of brave men.

The same attitude is being increasingly taken by the peace-loving Friends. "The young Quaker of the present day," writes one of them, "is so true to his inheritance—that of being allowed to act as his conscience dictates—that there are already many in the service, and that, too, with the fervent coöperation of their Quaker parents. . . . When one of these young Friends—now a trusted officer in the American infantry, who enlisted before war was declared by our Government—was challenged by a Quaker friend, he promptly replied: 'I am showing my regard for my Quaker ancestry and training in the fact that I cannot and will not allow war to stalk upon the earth unchecked. Only by meeting the Devil face to face can we hope to crush him.' "

Sir George Adam Smith in an American address stated that in Scotland 90 per cent of the ministers' sons of military age entered the army before conscription. Would it be strange if some fathers decided to go with them? He also said that of the sixty thousand Catholic priests engaged in war work in France, twenty-five thousand are fighting in the ranks. Some Chinese missionaries are serving behind the lines as officers of detachments of Chinese artisans and laborers. Other missionaries, however, and sons of missionaries are reported to have gone directly into military service. Our country's Roll of Honor contains the names of men like Captain Jewett Williams, an Episcopal rector and the son-in-law of Dr. David J. Barrows, Chancellor of the University of Georgia, who declined a chaplaincy, trained at Fort Oglethorpe, and was killed in action. Of recent graduates and members of the Yale School of Religion, forty-four are now in khaki. Of these nineteen are chaplains and Y. M. C. A. workers, while eighteen are in the regular army, one each in the British and Canadian armies, two in the Ambulance Corps, one in aviation and one in the navy. Already the School Roll of Honor bears one name, that of a young Englishman of rare promise, who died in the hospital from wounds received on the battlefields of France.

These men are following in the footsteps of ministers of other generations. Yale's records show that there is scarcely a campaign of note, or an important battle in American history, in which her sons among the clergy did not share the hardships and dangers of the soldier's lot. Besides the more than one hundred and thirty who served as chaplains, in the thick of the fight as well as in camp and hospital, are those who fought shoulder to shoulder with their parishioners. When the news of the approach of the enemy reached Thomas Brockway (1768) during service, he dismissed his congregation, shouldered his long gun, and marched away. Of John Cleaveland (1745) it is said that he preached all the men of his parish into the army and then went himself. They helped to take Louisburg in the campaign against Cape Breton Island. They marched in the Crown Point Expedition, fought at Ticonderoga, and shared with Wolfe the hardships of the campaign against Quebec. The record of the Revolutionary days is a stirring one. Edmund Foster (1778) joined the Minute Men on the sounding of the alarm in Lexington. Ebenezer Mosely (1763) enlisted in Israel Putnam's regiment, and with Joseph Badger (1785), who served with General Arnold in Canada, fought at the Battle of Bunker Hill. They were in the ranks at Germantown and at Monmouth. Samuel Eells (1765) was elected the captain of a company formed among his parishioners to aid General Washington, who was then retreating through New Jersey. Elisha Scott Williams (1775) crossed the Delaware in the boat with Washington, and is so depicted in Trumbull's painting. He also fought at the battles of White Plains, Trenton and Princeton, and shared with William Stone (1785) and Benjamin Wooster (1790) the hardships and sufferings at Valley Forge. Levi Lankton (1777) was present at Burgoyne's surrender.

In the Civil War this record is repeated. The ministers of Yale fought at Bull Run, South Mountain, Antietam, Fredericksburg, Chancellorsville, Gettysburg, the Wilderness, Spottsylvania and Cold Harbor. They rode with Sheridan's cavalry in the Army of the Potomac; they marched with General Sherman to the sea. Several, like Erastus Blakeslee (1863), well known for his services to the work of the Sunday school, rose to the rank of general.

Moses Smith (1852) entered in 1865 with the first troops into Richmond, while Samuel W. Eaton (1842), after fighting in some of the hardest battles, was present at Appomattox Court House on the surrender of General Lee.

In all this there is no thought of glorifying war, or of haloing the head of the minister who lays down his Bible to take up his bayonet. Quite the contrary. These fighting chaplains condemned war and hated it. They never proclaimed that organized slaughter was a sane method of settling international disputes or ethical questions. They would have marched to their own Calvaries gladly if this would have saved them from the horror of the task of the soldier and at the same time helped to bring in the Kingdom of God. But to their minds there was a time when a Christian ought to put up his sword, and another when his duty was to buy one. Devilishness is not usually overcome by allowing the Devil to have his way. If the powers of evil attempt by force to overthrow righteousness, righteousness may well by force oppose and thwart them; not that it may escape martyrdom, or vent its anger, but with the clear purpose of rescuing the evil doer from his devastating delusion, and of saving the most precious treasures of civilization from the axe of a vandalism, which can and ought to be restrained. The thought finds a crude but characteristic expression in Kipling's poem of Mulholland, the coarse sailor, who, in fulfilment of the vow made during a storm on the cattle-ship, goes back to preach religion to the brutal and unsympathetic crew:

I didn't want to do it, for I knew what I should get,
An' I wanted to preach religion, handsome an' out of the wet;
But the Word of the Lord were lain on me, and I done what I was set.

I have been smit and bruised, as warned would be the case,
An' turned my cheek to the smiter, exactly as Scripture says;
But following that, I knocked him down an' led him up to grace.

An' we have preaching on Sundays whenever the sea is calm,
An' I use no knife nor pistol, an' I never take no harm;
For the Lord abideth back of me to guide my fighting arm.

It is devoutly to be wished that it was never necessary for the preacher to use knife or pistol; but at present apparently there is no other means by which the smiter may be knocked down.

This teaching is what might be called, in Dr. Van Dyke's phrase, "Fighting for Peace." It is the kind of militant pacifism which Paul hints at. "If it be possible, as much as in you lieth, be at peace with all men." Sometimes it is not possible. It is neither wise nor saintly to attempt to negotiate with a tiger. It would be something worse than folly to allow the I. W. W. to dictate the economic policy of our country, or to suffer philosophical and practical anarchism to work its will with the law and order of the world. War as mere war deserves all the vitriolic epithets which have been heaped upon it. It is the scourge of scourges, the father of piracy and of murder, the mother of havoc, desolation and woe. It stands clearly revealed as "a monstrous crime, man's crowning imbecility and folly." But when through war the attempt is made to tear down law, overthrow justice and shackle the world's liberty, shall not war be met by war in order to preserve these priceless possessions, and perchance end all wars by rendering its mad champions powerless? No minister can be called Christian who does not hate war. But most of them hate still more the sinking of the Lusitania, the rape of Belgium, the massacre of the peaceful people of Armenia. They cannot with clear conscience sit still and watch the fulfilment of the plot of "the Potsdam gang" without striking a blow. Peace proposals from the successful marauders sound to them too much like Dr. Van Dyke's imaginary conversation between an outraged householder and his triumphant pacifistic burglar. It is not a question of Christ or Cæsar. There is something of the Sermon on the Mount in pacifist and militarist alike. But in the choice our ministers in the army have registered their vote for what seems to be by far the lesser of two evils. They with their fellows have chosen to tread the new Via Sacra, as the road is now called which made the salvation of Verdun possible; and today they stand facing the forces of autocracy, greed and military oppression, uttering that great battle cry which broke from the heart of France, "They shall not pass!"

Whatever the verdict of history upon this decision of brave men in the ministry, certain effects of the war upon them and upon their work are sure. These again are both good and evil. On the debit side of the ledger will be the loss of many in whose future service lay much of the hope and strength of the church. A large proportion of the best men, who were looking forward to the ministry, are in the training camps and trenches. Some may now be diverted to other callings; some will never come back. Their vacant places in the ranks will be saddening and for a time crippling. Great tasks which might have been done must needs be left undone. New Elishas will wear the prophet's mantle; but the memory of many a vanished face will waken the old cry upon their lips: "My father, my father, the chariots of Israel and the horsemen thereof!" If the church does not begrudge them, it will mourn them among its multitude of sons who

> laid the world away; poured out the red,
> Sweet wine of youth: gave up the years to be
> Of work and joy, and that unhoped serene
> That men call age; and those who would have been
> Their sons they gave—their immortality.

A second regrettable result in the minds of some will be the discrediting of the ministry. There have been too many un-Christian utterances from the pulpits of all lands, though we are naturally especially sensitive to those "made in Germany"; too many petty, superstitious prayers addressed to tribal deities as little like the God of Jesus as Moloch and Mars; too reckless dealing with "high literary explosives" on the part of preachers possessing neither the wisdom of Solomon nor the restraint of Paul; too flamboyantly patriotic utterances from orators who apparently forgot their obligations as citizens of heaven and makers of a new world. So far as the writer knows, there have been no blasphemies from the pulpits of the Allies equal to the saying of Pastor W. Lehmann: "The German soul is God's soul; it shall and will rule over mankind"; or that still more brutal and unblushing pronouncement of Pastor D. Baumgarten: "Whoever cannot prevail upon himself to approve from the bottom of his heart the sinking of the 'Lusitania,' whoever cannot conquer his sense of the gigantic cruelty to unnumbered innocent victims, and give himself up to the honest delight at the victorious exploit of German defensive power—him we judge to be no true German." But if none have descended to these depths of theological blindness and ethical madness, there has been a certain kinship with the spirit of the imprecatory psalms, used as convenient and refreshing outlets for pent-up tempers, together with more or less pagan treatment of ethical and religious questions, camouflaged with felicitous phrases, which lulled the listener with the assurance that the preacher was quoting from the Litany. All this has not redounded to the respect of the thoughtful for the pulpit, or for the leadership of men supposed to be specialists in the rules of right and teachers of the counsels of a fatherly God.

Furthermore, while the mass of Christian unity and coöperation has been unprecedented, there have been here and there expressions of denominational rivalries. It is not an inspiring spectacle when a few—and fortunately only a few—bigoted denominationalists are seen storming certain camps, not because the religious welfare of the soldiers is not being amply cared for, but because the accredited purveyor of their ecclesiastical shibboleth is not teaching his patois and peddling his wares. Neither our best laymen nor our wisest religious leaders have either patience or sympathy with modern denominational Pharisees. They recognize temperamental, psychological and national differences among fellow Christians, and are content that Quaker and High Churchman, shouting Methodist and dignified Scotch Presbyterian, Salvation Army lassie and devout Romanist should choose their own liturgy and polity, and go to heaven each in his own way. But to their minds, in everyday life usually and in camp life always, sectarian squabbling and doctrinal hair-splitting are merely rocks of stumbling and stones of offense; and whenever they witness, especially in war time, such wrangling in the porch of the sanctuary, they discount the utterances and even the calling of the minister, and, instead of entering the edifice and joining in the service, pass by on the other side.

Still more damning will be the accusation, made even by loyal sons of the church's own household, that not only has the ministry failed to prevent war, but that it neglected to mass its forces and measure its might in the great task. To reply to the charge in its undiscriminating, blunderbuss form is easy. Many ministers gave up their lives to the cause, notably in the various forms of the peace movement. Others proclaimed and urged a cure, which the laity declined to put into operation and the governments ignored. The prevention of war should have been the work of the educator, the lawyer, the scientist, the promoters of commerce and the prophets of international socialism as well as of the minister. If he is blameworthy, so are they. Men who love to sit in the seat of the scornful and jeer at Christianity should enlarge the scope of their humor. If, as G. K. Chesterton puts it, "Christianity has not been tried and found wanting; it has been found difficult and not tried," it is equally true that the ministry has not been trusted and found incompetent; it has been the herald of an unwelcome message and ignored. No one class in the community could work the miracle of a world-peace; it could be wrought only through the faith and works of all. To attribute to the ministers the failure to achieve it is in part fair; some of them are guilty. As Dean Hodges said of the much-discussed article, "Peter Sat by the Fire Warming Himself," the charges are richly deserved by those by whom they are deserved. In part, however, it is manifestly unfair; multitudes honestly tried. In part it is one of the greatest compliments ever paid them; for it suggests their power, acknowledges their leadership, and honors their task as the constructive statesmen of the world. No one ever before hinted that the clergy ought to have stopped the wars of Charlemagne or of Napoleon. During the Civil War neither the conflict nor the cause was laid at the minister's door. But in our day many clamor for priests after the order of Joshua as well as of Moses, men at the head of great bodies of Christian soldiers, who shall participate vigorously in domestic politics and international relations, until they actually bring in the reign of righteousness and of love and truth among men. As ministers we accept the compliment while we confess our sins and shortcomings. The burthen of having done the things we ought not to have done and of having left undone the things which we ought to have done is one that we carry shamefacedly but not exclusively. It is shared by all mankind.

But if the war kills some and discredits others, the credit page in the ledger looms large. The experiences and tasks of the present can hardly fail to make the manliest among us still more virile and vigorous. They will purge the leaders in every profession of all softness and sentimentalism, and lift them above a great danger in peace times, that of living a

ghastly, smooth life, dead at heart.

No sane and unprejudiced mind, possessing first-hand knowledge of the ministry, accepts as a representative of the profession the clergyman of the stage comedy and the popular novel. He may be a "sport," in the biological sense; but it would be equally easy to find as ludicrous and despicable examples in law, medicine or business. So far as the average, normal type is concerned, this popular clerical clown is a wretched caricature, possessing humor because endowed with the exaggeration and distortion of a political cartoon. But removing all such weaklings from the discussion, and granting that there are no more lax fellows, lolling through life, in the ministry than in any other profession, there is; as Donald Hankey points out, a certain directness and sternness in camp and military life which is singularly invigorating and even Christ-like. It stiffens a man's back to shoulder heavy burdens, trains the eye to face steadily and without flinching disagreeable and terrifying duties. It tenses muscles with great and glorious resolves. It girds up the loins for a race the issues of which are life and death, throttles any idea of sneaking sinuously through the world avoiding large and costly obligations, and at the end of the day's labor demands visible and tangible results. If any minister was in danger of becoming what Horace Greeley called "a pretty man," or what Holmes described as "a wailing poitrinaire," his experience as chaplain and as soldier will effectually cure him. We should have more prophets after the order of Amos as well as of Hosea when the men who have been under fire come home.

Such men will increasingly merit and possess the respect of laymen and of soldiers. Their lives have been knit together in the fellowship of suffering. Their bodies are inured to the same hardships, their faces lined with the same grim marks of dangers laughed at and of conquered pain. In the democracy of the trenches the sons of the Pilgrims and the immigrant sons of the slums have come to know and to understand one another. The pagan, illiterate dock-hand has fought shoulder to shoulder with the teacher of religion, trained in the first universities of our own and other lands. When such laymen attend plays like "The Hypocrites" or read novels like "The Pastor's Wife," they will never be persuaded that the clerical cartoons represent reality. Each will recall days in the dugouts and nights in the hospitals, when they came to know a different type of minister, a "beloved captain," who marched through the mire with song and laughter, and crept with them through the darkness and shadow of death in No Man's Land. An almost irresistible attraction will draw them to the churches of such ministers. To their leadership they will be inclined to render obedience; to their messages they will listen with respect. No scoffing jests at the minister will be allowed to go by them unchallenged. For the first time in their lives they have been brought into touch with the preachers of religion, and their hearts have burned within them while they talked with these disciples of Jesus by the way.

Furthermore, they will seek them out in the intercourse of ordinary fellowship. For the ministers have shown themselves friendly, approachable—no wan ascetics, no unhuman monks or superstitious other-worldlings, but jolly good fellows in camp life, sane and wholesome counsellors in times of perplexity, comforters in the hours of sorrow, efficient and tireless fellow workers; in brief, the best type of men among men. With such a minister there will be no social uneasiness, no camouflaged conversation during a pastoral visit or upon his entrance into the club. When he opens the front door, the father will not be so apt to call, "Mother, the dominie has come to see you!" It will be no longer the pastor who wishes to meet and to know the male parishioner; the male parishioner will be equally eager to meet and to know the pastor. One soldier phrased the difference in this way: "Well, sir, I like our services out here, and the church is all right; but our parson at home, sir—! You couldn't go to church or have anything to do with him!" All this will come to the minister as a reward for having realized the picture as painted by an English chaplain. "I like to think of the parish priest as fulfilling the Shakespearean stage direction—'Scene: a public place. Enter First Citizen';—for his ministry should mostly be spent neither in church nor in the homes of the faithful, but in public places; and he should be the First Citizen of his parish, sufficiently well known to all to be absolutely at home with each. . . . And so the word 'parson' will revert to its old proud meaning of 'persona,' and the priest will take in his parish a position analogous to that of the best chaplains in the army." That is the gift which true ministers have always coveted. Many have already won it, turning from the fascination of their studies "to waste time wisely in the market-place, gossiping like Socrates with all comers." After the war many more will possess it, having gladly paid the price.

To the spiritual practitioner, moreover, will have come increased skill in that most difficult of all arts, personal work. He will have had daily hospital training in ministering to the souls of men. He will speak their language, even their lingo, rather than what is to multitudes the unintelligible patois of the seminary Canaan. He will know not only his own theories but their difficulties and experiences in regard to a belief in immortality and the practice of prayer. Like Jesus at the well, he will have learned the method and value of gaining a point of contact in teaching. Formerly it was easy to discourse from the pulpit concerning the being and nature of God and to champion theories of the atonement. The prophet of the regiment will have learned what is far more difficult and more necessary—to persuade a man to follow the teaching and to practice the friendship of Jesus. That is his task, and he will have become efficient in its accomplishment—so to bring modern prodigals to themselves that they loathe the far country, and arise, and go home to their Father's house.

Another gain will be that of a deeper appreciation of denominational coöperation and an enlarged scope for the practice of it. Sectarian rivalries and ecclesiastical trivialities vanish in the trenches. Man-made walls between Christian brethren are crumbling. Petty partisanship becomes first ridiculous and then wicked in the light of the universal church's ambition. "We need a standard so universal," writes H. G. Wells, "that the plate-layer may say to the barrister or the duchess, or the Red Indian to the Limehouse sailor, or the Anzac soldier to the Sinn Feiner or the Chinaman, 'What are we two doing for it?' And to fill the place of that 'It' no other idea is great enough or commanding enough, but only the world Kingdom of God." The same buildings are now serving congregations of Jews, Protestants and Romanists.

Instant calls come when rabbis, priests, rectors, and representatives of every hue in the rainbow of Protestantism minister to men of other creeds and of no creed. Partisan politics in the field of pure religion are seen to be essentially irreligious; and chaplains of every ilk and kirk are working together like "Bill' and "Alf," two cockney soldiers, one of whom had lost a right arm and the other a left. They always sat side by side at the C. C. S. concerts "so as we can have a clap," as "Alf" put it. "Bill puts 'is 'and out, an' I smacks it with mine." Such men cannot come home and take part in the heresy trials and ecclesiastical hecklings of men whom at heart they recognize as Christian brethren. It is perfectly safe to prophesy that there will be more of church unity, and possibly more of uniformity, so far as this is desirable, when these apostles of hundreds of churches come home from the war.

With this enlarged coöperation will come also an enlarged ambition. The pastor who has been plodding along the familiar ways of an uninspiring parish will never be content to suffer his people to travel in the old ruts or to countenance out-worn and inefficient methods. That way, he now knows, lies ministerial melancholia and the present situation, something far worse than Lear's madness. His task, and that of his people, is nothing less than to transform their portion of the world into heaven. Singing and praying about it are good and necessary; but in the words of the old negro spiritual, it is perfectly patent that "Eberybody talks 'bout heaben ain't a-gwine dah," and the work of the church is to see to it that they go. Some of the strongest and most venturesome among the clergy, unwilling to turn back to the safe life after the thrill of the trenches, will seek adventure in pioneer work in our own land and abroad. Home missions will come as a challenge to men inured to danger and hardship. Foreign missions will have a new and poignant meaning for all the world. We knew before that the bubonic plague in Calcutta was a menace to San Francisco; we know now that the cult of militarism in a single group in Germany can crucify mankind. No chaplain will ever settle down into a parish as if it were a "pent-up Utica." No cultivation of individual piety will atone for the failure to Christianize society, leaven industry with the principles of Jesus, and convert from its Machiavellian heathendom and Bismarckian brutality the diplomacy of the old-time state. Nothing less than the ambition to take the world and its kingdoms for Christ can ever satisfy his soldiers; not, like the Central Powers, in order that they may be enslaved and exploited, but that they may know the fullness of joy and of freedom, and possess the true riches of that divine life which is life indeed.

Almost of necessity the experience at the front will simplify and vitalize the minister's message. For many all discussion of the future of unbaptized infants, and premillenialism, and the verbal inspiration of the Pentateuch had long ago lost interest. In the minds of others, matters regarded by some earnest Christians as of vital importance, like the Virgin Birth and the physical resurrection of Jesus, had ceased to function. To them Jesus would still be the unique Son of God, the divine Saviour of the world, whatever the method of his human generation; and he would still be alive, their unseen friend and present helper, whether or not his body had remained in the tomb. Belief or disbelief in such articles of faith would never transform a demon into a saint or a saint into a demon. Even to those accepting them, they had no visible effect upon character or upon the course of ordinary daily life. No soldiers ever asked about such scholastic problems as they faced going over the top on the morrow. In the hospital they never mentioned them, as they lay lonely and fearful on their beds of pain. But they did ask, or long to ask, had shyness not prevented them, about the treasures for which the heart hungers and to which religion alone holds the key.

"Dear Sir," wrote a wounded soldier to the chaplain of his battalion; "I often used to wish that you would talk seriously and privately to me about religion, though I never dared to ask you, and I must admit that I seemed to be very antagonistic when you did start." "I wish you'd tell me what you think about it, padre," said another. "Is there anything really afterwards? . . . I'd like you to tell me as man to man what you really think about it. Do we go on living afterwards in any sort of way or—!" He struck a match to light a cigarette. A gust of wind, which carried a gust of snow round our legs, blew the match out again. I daresay it was that which suggested his next words: "Or do we just go out? I know the creed," he went on. ". . . But that's not what I want. I want to know what you really believe yourself, as a man, you know."

Is there a God, and can we actually lead men to experience him and to grow like him? Is there any power in Jesus to save a brute and a drunkard, a selfish worldling and a contented prig, not from a hell of fire after death from which he is snatched by some theological transaction, but from his degradation and meanness in the present, until he is fit to be a husband and a father, a patriot and a friend? Are the fruits of the Christian spirit "love, joy, peace, long-suffering, goodness, meekness, faithfulness, and self-control," the qualities of character which alone can make heaven anywhere, and without which a potential Paradise would be transformed into an actual hell? Are the wages of sin death, or does the good man simply lose a deal of fun and prove himself to be a foolish prig and superstitious other-worlding? Does death end all, or are there many mansions in the Father's house? Such are the great questions; and to them Christianity has very definite answers, capable of being tried out in experience. In the past much of so-called religion has seemed to thoughtful minds remote from the facts of life, unreal, a bit queer if not abnormal. If the flames of war are purging it from such unrealities and abnormalities, the facts which lie at the heart of the world's faith are being saved, yet so as by fire. The Christianity of the camp is no pious sentimentalism, no sweet dream or unvirile worship of a "gentle Jesus." It is a living, indubitable experience, full of strength and of joy. Men are fighting to the death a thought and a purpose in the German armies which Prince Lichnowsky, their own ambassador to the British Court, characterized as "perfidy and the sin against the Holy Ghost"; and in that fight they hunger and thirst for the power of a religion of the Spirit, which—however the battle of bodies and of brute force may be decided—in God's good time is bound to win the day.

The last effect of the war upon the work and message of the minister will be to furnish it with a new dynamic. As he returns from the battle with sin in the trenches, he will find in the same battle at home William James' "moral equivalent for war." The call to arms has revealed the fact, seen in the success of the Student Volunteer Movement, that the church has not sufficiently appealed to men's latent heroism. The ordinary individual has revealed an enthusiastic readiness for high adventure and an almost limitless capacity for self-sacrifice, qualities upon which the work and preaching of the average parish made practically negligible demands. There was a contrast as noticeable as it was lamentable between the pompous phrases of certain militant hymns, sung chiefly by the choir, and the lack of ethical passion and aggressive righteousness on the part of the pews. There was too little doing of brave deeds and too much flabby irresolution and orthodox laziness. Christianity seemed to act as a narcotic rather than a stimulant. Any preacher might say to any congregation with perfect safety, "Ye have not yet resisted unto blood, striving against sin."

For the chaplain fresh from the front all this will be changed. Not only will he be the flaming apostle of a new enthusiasm; his church will have been saved from the old lethargy and lukewarmness of Laodicea, the minds of his people purged from the *dolce far niente* pietism, which dreamed sweet dreams while the wreckers of the world prepared for war. For today religion stands revealed as the greatest of all adventures. Christianity is history's crowning crusade. The greed, the brutality, the imbecile and devilish lawlessness, which have revelled in an orgy of spiritual vandalism, are not peculiar to war. They have long been with us, in city and in country, in the slums and on the avenue, among peoples supposed to be civilized and enjoying the blessings of an era of prosperity and of peace. It was an amazed world, rudely roused from its comfortable slumbers, which found these forces organized for battle; it will be a bloody and dishevelled but determined and aggressive world that, when our men have laid aside their khaki, will strive to hold them in the ranks of an equally fearless and fighting army, which will never retreat from its trenches until these enemies of the world's peace and happiness are driven from the field. Men who hated dirt and discomfort, blood and vermin, have endured and laughed at them for the sake of their cause and their country. When the call comes to carry on the same fight in the homeland, such heroic souls will scarcely decline to sacrifice something of their peace and comfort, or to attack the forces entrenched in saloon and dive and political cave of Adullam, because in the struggle they may be shorn of delights and dollars, know the shame and agony of temporary defeat, and as victors find themselves with mire upon their garments and blood upon their hands. "Never was there a religion more combative than Christianity," wrote Bernhardi. That is false as the apostle of carnage meant it; but it is true to the disciple of Jesus, who has heard Paul's summons to don the full panoply of the Christian armor, and who so loves the Lord as to hate evil with the just but terrible wrath of the Lamb. Here is a new dynamic, an irresistible appeal, which should and must be utilized by the minister. If the Christian Church is an army with the greatest of fights on its hands, there will be a place for the soldier. With the church service of the religious slacker he may be pardoned if he declines to have anything to do.

T. R. Glover in "The Jesus of History" has said that the Christian conquered because he out-lived and out-thought and out-died the pagan. It is beginning to dawn upon the ministry that we must out-fight him, if he is to be conquered in our day. The clergy have seen their opportunity pictured in the words with which John Masefield in "Gallipoli" has told the story of the final attack upon Suvla Bay. "There was the storm," he writes, "there was the crisis, the one picked hour, to which this death and agony . . . had led. Then was the hour for the casting off of self, and a setting aside of every pain and longing and sweet affection, a giving up of all that makes a man to the something which makes a race, and a going forth to death resolvedly to help out their brothers high above in the shell bursts and the blazing gorse." The thousands who are responding to that call are the priests of today and the prophets of tomorrow. They can cry to us, with their fellow soldiers, living and dead, in the words of Lawrence Binyon:

O you that still have rain and sun,
  Kisses of children and of wife,
And the good earth to tread upon,
  And the mere sweetness that is life,
Forget not us who gave all these
For something dearer, and for you!
Think in what cause we crossed the seas!
Remember, he who fails the challenge
Fails us, too.

Now in the hour that shows the strong—
  The soul no evil powers affray—
Drive straight against embattled Wrong:
  Faith knows but one, the hardest, way.
Endure; the end is worth the throw.
Give, give; and dare, and again dare!
On, to the Wrong's great overthrow!
We are with you, of you; we the pain and
Victory share.

VI

THE EFFECT OF THE WAR UPON RELIGIOUS EDUCATION

LUTHER ALLAN WEIGLE

THE term "religious education" stands for two ideas that are ultimately one: for the inclusion of religion in our educational program, and for the use of educational methods in the propagation of religion from generation to generation.

Over seventy years ago, Horace Bushnell pointed out the folly of reliance upon the revival method of dealing with the children of Christian homes, and urged the educational method of Christian nurture. He did more than any other one man to determine the present trend in religious education. Yet his work was prophetic; it took fifty years more of "ostrich nurture," as he called it, to reveal to Christian people generally the full truth of his position.

The past twenty years, however, have witnessed a great movement among the Protestant churches of America toward clearer aims and better methods in religious education. A situation had developed that bid fair to let religion drop out of the education of American children. Changed social, economic and industrial conditions had transferred to the school many of the educational functions once fulfilled by the home, and had wrought a change in the forms of family religion. The public schools had become increasingly secular in aim, in control, and in material taught. The development of science and philosophy in independence of religion had made it possible for college students to get the idea that religion is not a significant part of the life and culture of the time. The Sunday school, indeed, was at work, teaching children of God and his will. But its curriculum was ungraded, its teachers untrained, and its instruction limited to one period of half an hour in each week.

Roughly speaking, the beginning of the present century may be taken as the date when the Christian people of America began to awake to the danger involved in this situation. As early as the late eighties, President W. R. Harper, then Woolsey Professor of Biblical Literature at Yale, had organized the American Institute of Sacred Literature, and had begun to publish a graded series of Inductive Studies in the Bible. In 1900, under his leadership, the University of Chicago published the first of its present series of Constructive Studies, which provides text-books for a graded curriculum of religious education. In 1903, the Religious Education Association was organized, its membership drawn from the whole of the United States and Canada, and its purpose declared to be threefold: "To inspire the educational forces of our country with the religious ideal; to inspire the religious forces of our country with the educational ideal; and to keep before the public mind the ideal of religious education, and the sense of its need and value." In 1908, the International Sunday School Association authorized its Lesson Committee to construct and issue a graded series of Sunday school lessons in addition to the uniform series which it had issued year after year since 1872. In 1910 the Sunday School Council of Evangelical Denominations was organized, a mark of the more definite assumption by the several denominations of responsibility for the educational work of their Sunday schools and for the training of teachers. In 1912, the Council of Church Boards of Education came into being, which has devoted its energies thus far mainly to coöperative effort in behalf of Christian colleges and for the religious welfare of college and university students generally.

These are but a few outstanding factors in a movement greater far than any single organization or group of organizations. There has been an awakening of the spirit of education in religion. Sunday schools the country over have been graded, and here and there week-day schools of religion have been begun; problems of curriculum, method and organization have been studied and graded curricula devised; classes and schools for the training of teachers have been organized; and attempts of various sorts have been made to correlate public and religious education. Churches in general have come to see that they have an educational as well as a religious function in the community, and that there is a sense in which they share with the public school a common task. The public school can teach the "three R's," the sciences, arts and vocations; the church must teach religion. Both are needed if the education of our children is to be complete. Many churches are employing paid teachers of religion and directors of religious education. Courses in religious education have been organized and professorships of religious education established in colleges and theological seminaries. "The Educational Ideal in the Christian Ministry" was the subject of the Lyman Beecher Lectures on Preaching, in the Yale School of Religion, a few years ago. The young men who are entering the Christian ministry in these days are being trained, not simply to preach and to care for a parish, but to teach and to direct the educational work of a church.

The immediate effect of the war has been to retard this movement in some degree. Preoccupation with the war itself and with more immediately pressing needs, has made more difficult the work of the churches in this as in other respects. Churches that had planned new buildings for their schools are postponing their erection till the war is over. Training classes for teachers are harder to keep up. Ministers are going into war service; and those who stay at home are doing double work or more. Churches, like business houses and factories, have found their organizations broken by the departure of members of military age. Many of their best teachers and leaders have gone to war; and it is not easy, in these days of urgency and stress, to discover others to take their places.

It is probable, however, that a deeper effect of the war will be to intensify our sense of the importance of religious education and to clarify the church's educational program, in point both of content and method. This conviction rests upon these fundamental facts: that the world is achieving democracy; that it believes in and relies upon education; that it is experiencing what may prove to be a renewal of religion.

Education, democracy, religion—these three, we have long professed and more or less fully believed, belong together. The full life of each of the three is bound up in that of the other two.

Education without religion is incomplete and abortive; it falls short of that life more abundant which is education's goal. Religion without education lacks intelligence and power, and condemns itself to what Horace Bushnell called conquest from without, as contrasted with growth from within.

Democracy without education cannot long hold together or be saved from mediocrity and caprice. Education without democracy perpetuates caste divisions, or else breeds discontent and class hatred.

Democracy without religion is doomed to fail; and religion without democracy cannot realize the Fatherhood of God and the brotherhood of man.

These, I say, are familiar convictions. They are natural to Protestantism; they have entered into the very making of America. Yet just these old convictions are gaining a new force and a deeper meaning in and through the experiences of these years of war. The struggle for democracy is not only leading us to a new comprehension of the meaning of democracy itself; it is helping us to understand better both education and religion.

It does not lie within the limits of this paper to canvass the wider and deeper meaning of democracy which is opening before us. The messages and addresses of President Wilson have interpreted that meaning not simply to America but to the world. No one yet knows the full promise of life after the war, when Pan-Germanism shall have been not only balked but destroyed. The democracy for which we fight to make the world safe will be a chastened, changed, completer democracy. It will be a democracy between nations as well as within nations, for the doctrine of the irresponsible, beyond-moral sovereignty of the state must return to the perdition whence it came. It will be a democracy applied more fully to the whole of life, social, economic and industrial as well as political. It will be a democracy of completer citizenship, that gives place to women as to men. It will be a democracy of duties as well as of rights.

The world is acquiring a new conscience. Just as the nineteenth century made slavery abhorrent to the moral sense of men in general, the twentieth century will likely be looked back to as the time when the world's conscience decided that the exploitation of man by man is wrong. The general moral sense of men has not been over-tender on this point hitherto. They have checkmated the exploiter if they could, as they did checkmate Napoleon, but they have not always, or even usually, looked upon him as a wrong doer. It required Germany's attempts at conquest and subjugation to wake the world to the absolute wrong of that monstrous thing—that one man should use another as a mere means to his own pleasure or aggrandizement, or that one people should so determine the destiny of another people.

Here lies the supreme moral issue of the war. Shall the world, which has become a neighborhood, organize itself into a great community of mutual respect, good will and brotherhood, or shall its structure be that of restless orders of exploiters and exploited? It is over-familiar; yet, lest we forget, hear some random verses from various Pan-Germanist scriptures: "Not to live and let live, but to live and direct the lives of others, that is power." "To compel men to a state of right, to put them under the yoke of right by force, is not only the right but the sacred duty of every man who has the knowledge and the power." "The German race is called to bind the earth under its control, to exploit the natural resources and the physical powers of man, to use the passive races in subordinate capacity for the development of its *Kultur*." "Life is essentially appropriation, injury, conquest of the strange and weak, suppression, severity, obtrusion of its own forms, incorporation at the least, and in its mildest form exploitation."

Contrast with this the words of Jesus: "Ye know that they who are accounted to rule over the Gentiles lord it over them; and their great ones exercise authority over them. But it is not so among you: but whosoever would become great among you, shall be your minister; and whosoever would be first among you, shall be servant of all." The present struggle is not merely between democracy and autocracy as rival systems of government. It is a struggle between opposed philosophies of life. Nietzsche was more consistent than the Kaiser who has followed him, for Nietzsche did not claim to be a Christian. He frankly proposed a "transvaluation of values" which would do away with the religion of Jesus as fit only for slaves. That proposed transvaluation of values the Kaiser is trying to bring about, however piously he may lie about it or claim God's partnership in his enterprise.

Prophecies are always hazardous; never more so than now. The outlook for religion has been discussed both by puzzled pacifists and by facile forecasters of the fulfilment of their own wishes. One may perhaps question whether there will be any *one* trend of the churches in the immediate future. Yet this is clear: that the interests of democracy and the interests of true religion are ultimately one. We may confidently expect the churches of tomorrow to realize this more fully, not simply in the ideals they preach, but in the temper and quality of their own life. *One effect of the war upon religious education, undoubtedly, will be to make it more democratic in aim, content and method.*

Education in general will become more democratic. The experiences of these years are helping us to understand education and to estimate its values. Our eyes are being opened to the diametrical difference between democratic and undemocratic education. We have come to see that the latter may be as great a menace to the world as the former is a vital resource.

The time was, not long ago, when Germany was deemed the school-master of the world. German efficiency and German obedience to authority were seen to be the products of German teachers and German schools. In methods of teaching and in school organization, as well as in ideals of scholarship, the world sought to follow Germany. If here and there one objected that German education seemed to sacrifice the individual to the system and to beget an obedience too implicit, we felt that it was only because the Germans are such docile, pious, family folk, and we rather chided ourselves for our rougher ways and for that self-will that made us unholily thankful that we had been born in a freer land.

But now the character of German education stands revealed. We are no longer as hopeful as we once were of the possible success of an appeal to the German people over the heads of their military masters. They seem on the whole to like the kind of government they have, and to want to be exploited by Prussia. They are perilously near to what Mr. H. G. Wells has given as his definition of damnation—satisfaction with existing things when existing things are bad. They are experiencing what Mr. Edmond Holmes has called the Nemesis of docility.

And it is their system of education that has brought about this result. If the German people are damned to satisfaction with irresponsible autocracy and fatuous docility, their schools have damned them. For a century, German education has been at work to breed the present world-menace. The German schools have made the German people what they are. They have sought to develop habits of mind rather than free intelligence; they have valued efficiency in a given task above initiative and power to think for oneself. They have set children in vocational grooves and molded them to pattern. They have educated the few to exert authority, and have trained the many to obey. They have nurtured the young upon hatred of other peoples; and, much as the Jews of old awaited the Messiah, they have lived and labored in expectation of "The Day." They have exalted Vaterland into a religion, and have degraded God into a German tutelary deity. The German schools have welded the German people into a compact, efficient, military machine. The desires of the State are their desires; the Kaiser's will is their will.

We have been following false gods, therefore, in so far as we have sought to shape our schools upon German models. "The German teacher *teaches*," wrote one of our great educators some years ago, in criticism of our American way of giving to children text-book assignments which they are expected to study for themselves; yet the text-book method, fumblingly as we have so often used it, gives better training in initiative and intelligence than the German teacher's dictation methods. Professor Charles H. Judd has recently pointed out the confusion and waste of time brought about by the fact that our eight-year elementary school was modeled upon the German Volksschule, which is a school for the lower classes, and not intended to lead on to higher education. Our purpose, on the contrary, is to maintain for every American child an open ladder through elementary school, secondary school and college to the university; and to that purpose a six-year period of elementary education is much better adapted—a plan which many of our school systems have adopted within the last decade. We need better vocational education in this country and better systems of vocational guidance; but we are becoming clear that these must not be of the German sort, that compel a choice before the teens.

Education in a democracy must be education for democracy; and education for democracy must itself be democratic in content and method. Such education practices and aims at intelligence rather than habit of mind. It trains its pupils to think and choose for themselves. It prizes initiative above conformity, responsibility above mere efficiency, social good will above unthinking obedience.

Such education is more difficult, of course, than education of the undemocratic type. We shall at times be tempted to fall back into the ways of the German schools in some respect or other, because they represent the line of least resistance in education. Specious arguments will be presented in favor of these ways by short-sighted "practical" men. Education of the German type is more efficient, they will say; it is more direct and practical; it brings more immediate results. It is more patriotic, moreover, they will insist; it better serves the ends of authority; it makes people more prosperous and contented, each in his appointed niche. But such arguments, we may well hope, will no longer win the uncritical assent that they have sometimes found. German education may be more efficient in the fulfilment of its end than American education—but what an end it has sought and reached! In the moment of our temptation to undemocratic short cuts in education, we shall henceforth look to the Germany of yesterday and today, and shall be strengthened to resist. Her ways are not our ways. Her schools cannot be ours. Education must mean to America something quite different from what it has meant to Germany.

The contrast between democratic and undemocratic types of education is as great with respect to religion as with respect to the rest of life. Germany has been most careful to maintain religion as a subject of instruction in her schools. But the content of this instruction in religion has been intellectualistic and formal. It has pressed upon German children a body of historical facts, moral precepts and theological dogmas; but it has not begotten the freedom of inward spiritual initiative. State-controlled, it has bent religion to state uses, and has in time begotten a generation who can believe in the "good old German God."

Religious education in America has been and will be more democratic. Horace Bushnell used to say that the aim of all education is the emancipation of the child. We teach and train our children in order that they may in due time be set free from paternal discipline. We fail in the religious education of our children if our teaching does not result in their final emancipation from a religion of mere authority and convention and their growth into a religion of the spirit. We aim, not simply to win their assent to a given body of beliefs or to attach them to the church as a saving institution, but to help them to become men and women who can think and choose for themselves. The Protestant principle of the universal priesthood of believers involves democracy in religion. And just as democracy can look forward only to failure unless it can educate its citizens, Protestantism will fail unless it can educate men and women fit to stand on their own feet before God, able to understand his will and ready to enter intelligently and effectively into the common human enterprises of Christian living.

A second effect of the war, closely related to this, is that religious education will concern itself more directly with life, and will put less emphasis upon dogma, especially upon those refinements of creed which have operated divisively in the life of the Christian Church. Its method will be more vital, and less intellectualistic. Instead of proceeding upon the assumption that true belief comes first and that right life is the expression of prior belief, it will recognize that adequate insight and true belief are more often the result of right life and action. "If any man willeth to do his will, he shall know of the teaching." If this be true of adults, it is even more true of children. Our plans of religious education will first seek to influence the life, and will deal with beliefs as an explanation of life's purposes and motives and an interpretation of its realities and values.

If they will realize this primacy of life, the Christian churches stand in the presence of a great opportunity. The experiences of these years have shown us how much more of Christian living there is in the world than bears the label. Religion is being tested, stripped of sham and embroidery, and reduced to reality. And there are being revealed breadths and depths of real religion that we had not understood. There is a vast amount of inarticulate religion actually moving the lives of men which the churches may lift to the level of intelligent and articulate belief if they will but approach it with understanding and a willingness to be taught as well as to teach.

In Jesus' story of the last judgment, there is surprise all around. Both those on the right hand and those on the left stand fully revealed to themselves for the first time, it seems. "Lord, when saw we thee . . ." they cry on both sides. This war has constituted such a judgment day. A great moral issue has stood out, sharp, clean-cut and clear. It has set men on the right hand and on the left. It brooks no moral hyphenates; it permits no half-allegiance, either to country or to God. Beneath all pretense and profession, it lays bare the real man. It reveals the hidden qualities of nations. There have been many surprises. It has shown far more of evil in the world that we had deemed possible; but it has shown, too, far more of goodness and courage and true religion than we had thought was there.

Evil is here—real, powerful, poignant, and more unutterably bad than the farthest stretch of imagination had hitherto conceived that evil could be. Since the world began it was never so full of pain and suffering in body and mind, of needless death and of mothers brave but broken-hearted. And most of this is the result of supreme moral evil, the work of a power deliberately seeking world-domination and exploitation of the rest of mankind, even though it involve the extermination of other peoples, determined to use any methods that bid fair to bring about this result, and organizing deceit and lust and murder as the instruments of *Schrecklichkeit.*

But goodness is here too—strong, calm, cheerful, brave, self-devoting goodness. These years of war have revealed to us the supreme power of the human spirit to endure pain, to resist evil, and to count all else naught for sake of the right in which it believes and the good upon which its heart is set.

This goodness does not always call itself Christian, be it granted, or even know itself to be such. A chaplain in the English army writes: "There is in the army a very large amount of true religion. It is not, certainly, what people before the war were accustomed to call religion, but perhaps it may be nearer the real thing. It is startling, no doubt, and humiliating to find out how very little hold traditional Christianity has upon men. . . . So far as I am able to estimate, we are faced now with this situation, *a Christian life* combined with *a pagan creed.* For while men's conduct and their outlook are to a large extent unconsciously Christian, their creed (or what they think to be their creed) most emphatically is not. . . . Nevertheless I feel that out here one is very near to the spirit of Christ. There is a general wholesomeness of outlook, a sense of justice, honor and sincerity, a readiness to take what comes and *carry on,* a power of endurance genuinely sublime, a light-heartedness and cheeriness (nearly always, I believe, put on for the sake of other people), a generosity and comradeship which are obviously Christ-like."[1]

There is strength and goodness at home, too. We had become accustomed in late years to hear it said that the churches were losing their hold upon the people of America. Whether or not that be true, the war has begun to reveal to America, as it has to our Allies, the depth and power of the real moral and spiritual life beneath the surface. Granted that we are witnessing no widespread evangelistic stirrings, no indications of a great revival. It seems probable, indeed, that the itinerant evangelists who had

1 "The Church in the Furnace," pp. 53-54.

lately become the fashion among us, have passed the heyday of their power. Neither are the "prophetic" folk who misunderstand their Bibles so persistently and look so confidently for the second coming of the Lord, winning an assent at all commensurate with their effort. But there is a vast amount of quiet, sensible, devoted Christian living in America. There is more of genuine religion among us than we had realized. That religion, for the most part inarticulate, and hardly knowing itself to be Christian, is finding expression in action. The spirit in which America entered the war; the high moral aims which President Wilson, interpreter yet leader of his people, has set before the world; the quiet, matter-of-fact and matter-of-duty way in which the principle of selective service was accepted and carried out as democracy's method of mobilizing its power; the coöperation and the giving; the uncomplaining solemn pride of homes that have already made the supreme sacrifice—these are but the first evidences in America of a moral virility, a real religion, which, we may confidently hope, will strengthen us, with our Allies, not only to carry on to victory, but to resist the victor's temptations.

Will this deep, elemental, common religion of America come to understand itself, and to recognize its fundamentally Christian character? The answer to that question lies with the churches. And there are clear indications that many of them, at least, will not fail to realize and meet their opportunity.

Not that we shall do without dogmas. Religion cannot maintain itself as mere ethics. It is a way of living; but a way of living that justifies itself by a way of believing about God and duty and immortality. The point is, that in the natural order of growth life has a certain priority to belief, action to full understanding. And that certainly is the order of growth involved in the present situation.

As the churches share in the expanding and deepening common life and bring their beliefs to bear upon it, in interpretation of its ultimate motives and hopes, there will be growth on both sides.

Men elementally Christian in action will come to know what they believe; and on the other hand the churches themselves will discern more clearly which of their customs and beliefs are relevant to the real issues of life and function in essential ways. Our creeds will become simpler, but more vital. And that will make possible a closer unity of the churches. One may well question both the possibility and the desirability of a complete obliteration of denominational lines. We may always have and need denominational loyalty just as we shall always have and need patriotism. But denominational loyalties can be incorporated into a higher loyalty to the inclusive fellowship of Christ's Church as a whole, just as national loyalties, we now see, can and must be incorporated into a higher loyalty to humanity which will be given expression and body in a world-wide League of Nations.

We may expect religious education after the war, again, to be more fully Christian in its conception of God as well as in its view of life.

Jesus, so far as we know, never used the word "democracy." Yet just such a democratic world-community as we are now beginning in a practical way to understand and strive for, he taught and lived and died for. Christianity's ultimate ideal is no longer a mere ideal. It has become an actual political and social program and possibility.

"The brotherhood of mankind must no longer be a fair but empty phrase," wrote President Wilson to Russia; "it must be given a structure of force and reality. The nations must realize their common life and effect a workable partnership to secure that life against the aggressions of autocratic and self-pleasing power." The world's choice is between "Utopia or hell," is Mr. Wells' striking phrase, which he expounds in a remarkable article in *The New Republic* on "The League of Nations." "Existing states," he says, "have become impossible as absolutely independent sovereignties. The new conditions bring them so close together and give them such extravagant powers of mutual injury that they must either sink national pride and dynastic ambitions in subordination to the common welfare of mankind or else utterly shatter one another. It becomes more and more plainly a choice between the League of free nations and famished men looting in search of non-existent food amidst the burning ruins of our world. In the end I believe the common sense of mankind will prefer a revision of its ideas of nationality and imperialism to the latter alternative."

Mr. Wells is right. The proposal to establish a league of nations presents itself in our day as a matter of plain common sense. Yet if there is one lesson written with perfect clearness on the pages of history, it is that common sense alone cannot save the world from the tragedies of error, self-will and sin, and that common sense motived by self-interest will in the end defeat itself. In his Lyman Beecher Lectures on Preaching, Dr. Henry Sloane Coffin has called our attention to the remarkable prophecy of the present world war made by Frederick W. Robertson in a sermon preached at Brighton on January 11, 1852, addressed to a generation that glorified commerce as the guarantor of world unity and sought to establish morality upon a basis of enlightened self-interest. The passage cannot be quoted too often, nor too firmly impressed upon the minds of the present generation, for there were those among us who, even up until the invasion of Belgium, kept protesting that there could be no war in a world so bound together by economic and commercial ties, and there are those now who find in such interests the only durable basis for world reconstruction. "Brethren," said Robertson, "that which is built on selfishness cannot stand. The system of personal interest must be shriveled to atoms. Therefore, we who have observed the ways of God in the past are waiting in quiet but awful expectation until He shall confound this system as He has confounded those which have gone before, and it may be effected by convulsions more terrible and bloody than the world has yet seen. While men are talking of peace and of the great progress of civilization, there is heard in the distance the noise of arms, gathering rank on rank, east and west, north and south, and there come rolling toward us the crushing thunders of universal war. . . . There is but one other system to be tried, and that is the cross of Christ—the system that is not to be built upon selfishness nor upon blood, not upon personal interest, but upon love."

If Wells has stated the world's alternative, Robertson has shown the way of final and permanent right decision. To common sense must be added love. The brotherhood of man must be established upon a common acknowledgment of the Fatherhood of God. The world community can ultimately be motived by nothing less than the life within the hearts of men of the God whom they come to know through Jesus Christ.

This means both that the world must become more religious, and that religion must become more fully Christian. We can no longer believe in any God less great or less good than the God whom Jesus Christ reveals. However much it may be tempted to the lower view from time to time, we may reasonably expect that henceforth the world is done with belief in a mere tribal or national God. The supreme and inmost bond of the world community can be nothing other and nothing less than the Father of our Lord Jesus Christ, who regards all men as his children and who steadfastly seeks, with them and through them, the good of all.

Religious education after the war will be more democratic, more immediately concerned with life, more fully Christian. In so interpreting the present situation, we have had in mind especially the more or less formal religious education in the church and the church school. The same tendencies will influence the more informal and indirect religious education of children in the family. We have reason, indeed, to hope for a strengthening of family ties and a renewal of family religion. The sacrifices of these days are rendering relationships very precious that in a more careless, unthinking time we had accepted as a matter of course. And it is entirely possible that victory may wait until in America, as in England and France, there are few families that do not live in closer fellowship with the unseen world because their sons are there. The gradual disintegration of family life which the past half century has witnessed was but incidental to a rapid change in social, economic and industrial conditions. There is reason to expect that the family will so adjust its life to these conditions as to maintain its character as a social group, wherein genuine democracy and true religion may be propagated from generation to generation by that sharing of interests, occupations and affections which is the most potent and vital of all educational methods. That it should so adjust itself and so fulfill its primary educational function, should be a matter of the utmost concern to both Church and State, for it is hard to conceive how either the Christian religion or a democratic society could maintain itself without the aid of the family.

VII

FOREIGN MISSIONS AND THE WAR, TODAY AND TOMORROW

HARLAN P. BEACH

It might seem to the uninformed reader that foreign missions and war have nothing in common; for "what communion hath light with darkness? And what concord hath Christ with Belial?" Fuller knowledge of the varied work of missions and of its many helpful contributions to African, Asiatic and Oceanic peoples would remove this misapprehension. Professor Coolidge, of Harvard, suggests some important points of contact between missions and the less developed races, particularly of the enterprise as carried on today in contrast with its earlier objectives.[1] How the races of mission fields that have been thus affected are contributing to the war at home and in the trenches, Dr. Arthur J. Brown has described most vividly in a paragraph upon the cosmopolitan composition of the allied forces at the front.[2] Missionary periodical files abound in references to the war's inroads upon missionary enterprises, and to the important mediating work of missions. A great volume of testimony would show that while missionaries still regard the upbuilding of the mind and the saving of souls as fundamentally desirable, the enterprise affects every phase of the personal and community life of the peoples to which it ministers.

Statistics of the missionary situation at the beginning of the war reveal the extent and scope of present-day foreign missions.

[1] A. C. Coolidge, "The United States as a World Power," p. 329.

[2] F. Lynch, "President Wilson and the Moral Aims of the War," New York, 1918, pp. 50-51.

In the latest full collection of such statistics,[3] one finds a series of tables devoted to "General and Evangelistic" data, to "Educational" activities of missions, and to "Medical and Philanthropic" enterprises conducted by missionaries. It is impracticable to present the totals of the seventy-two columns, suggestive of the many subordinate activities of missions; a few items will indicate the more important contacts established between the Protestant churches of Christendom and the fifty fields which their missions have touched in many helpful ways. In these mission countries 351 Protestant societies had as their foreign staff 24,039 missionaries, including 13,719 women workers and wives. Stationed at 4,094 towns and villages, they directed the activities of a native staff of 109,099 and of 26,210 churches, the communicant membership of which was 2,408,900, with 1,423,314 others under religious instruction. In their elementary schools were 1,699,775 pupils, while in secondary schools were 218,207, and in the colleges and universities 15,636 students were enrolled. In theological and Bible training institutions 10,588 were preparing for the Christian leadership of the churches. Their industrial schools had an enrolment of 10,125, and their normal students numbered 7,504. Mission hospitals and dispensaries were presided over by 1,589 physicians and trained nurses, aided by a native staff of 2,336. In the year reported, 3,107,755 individuals were treated, in single visits or during prolonged residence in hospitals. Orphanages numbered 245, with 9,736 inmates, and 39 leper homes sheltered 1,880 unfortunate outcasts. Such an exhibit, incomplete as it is, will indicate the manifold tendrils which have bound Christian missionaries to the hearts of the nations; and if Roman Catholic statistics for this date were available,[4] the importance of missions as a steadying and reconstructive force at present and in post-bellum readjustments would be even more manifest.

[3] Beach and St. John, "World Statistics of Christian Missions," 1916, pp. 59-61.

[4] For the year 1913, see P. K. Streit, "Atlas Hierarchicus," summarized in "World Statistics of Christian Missions," pp. 103-104.

In discussing the war as affecting missions, only a few outstanding facts can be mentioned. Practically all of the mission world has taken sides in the tremendous conflict, most of these nations declaring for the Allies. Many of them have generously contributed the means and man force to hasten the day of peace. In 1917 nearly half a million from India were enlisted, of whom 285,200 were combatants and the rest were employed behind the lines in multifarious tasks. As a result of the recent conference at Delhi, it is hoped that another half million may be secured this year,[5] thus giving that Empire the numerical precedence among Britain's dominions. From North China alone some 135,000 laborers are serving the British forces in varied ways. "They come, also, from Morocco, Algeria, Tunis and the jungles of Senegal; from Madagascar and Tahiti, and several hundred thousand from French Indo-China and China proper. Black, yellow and white, East and West, educated and ignorant, progressive and backward, are laboring side by side."[6] So important is it that these polyglot assistants and warriors should be cared for in a Christian way that many missionaries have been called away from their distant fields to a manifold ministry to their adopted countrymen behind the trenches. Many of these recruits are Christian volunteers, especially so in the Indian contingent.

The effects of this European Armageddon upon the mission fields themselves has been less harmful than had been expected and more advantageous than was anticipated. German missions have been affected most among the Protestants, and among Roman Catholics France has been the chief sufferer. In the latter country there is no exemption for either Protestant or Catholic ministers of military age. Missions-Direktor Axenfeld of Berlin, in a recent publication,[7] states that German Protestant work in Africa has

[5] London *Times*, May 16, 1918.

[6] Personal letter from an investigator in France, May 29, 1918.

[7] "Das Kriegserlebnis der deutschen Mission in Lichte der Heiligen Schrift" as quoted in *The Missionary Review of the World* for June, 1918, pp. 423-424.

been practically disrupted, in India crippled by enforced withdrawals, in smaller British colonies similarly weakened by the expulsions, and permitted to go on with restrictions in other parts of Asia and North America. According to later information, about 400 German Protestant missionaries and missionary candidates are in military service, 68 are in hospitals, 120 are prisoners of war in various countries, and about 1,000 missionaries are still working in various fields. Referring to the *Zeitschrift für Missionswissenschaft*, in the files for 1915 and 1916, one learns that 3,000 Catholic missionaries are estimated to have been called to the colors, and that in 1916 there were 2,336 serving in the army. French Protestant missions, with a much smaller force abroad, have suffered in similar proportion; so that in French and German mission fields the personnel has been greatly reduced, limited, or has been obliterated entirely. British missions have likewise sent to the colors many of their best men from the field and the candidate list, while a number have been transferred from field service to work among their constituency in Mesopotamian and French camps. Relatively few native Christian leaders have enlisted.

The Christian communities in mission lands have suffered in various ways through the war. The removal of supervising missionaries in part—almost wholly in the case of German societies—has left many flocks without their chief shepherds. Great as has been this loss, it has wrought a greater benefit in churches whose native leaders thus have been brought to the front and have proved to their congregations that the church was so far indigenous as to survive the withdrawal of missionaries. To help their pastors, the people have undertaken responsibilities which without this necessity would not have been borne, thus developing unsuspected gifts and engendering hope for the future. During the war, evangelistic campaigns, largely participated in by the native church, have been carried on in a number of countries and with marked success.

Participation in the great conflict by the Christians and non-

Christians of mission lands has had mixed results. On the one hand, any delusion as to the civilization and attitudes of so-called Christian countries has been dissipated by the undreamed of savagery and international hatred which they have seen. This has led to opposition to missionaries on the fields, especially in Persia and in Morocco, where a Moslem said to Dr. Kerr: "Why don't you turn your attention to Christians? With all our faults, we have some religion left, but the Christians have none." On the other hand, it has revealed to the peoples so aiding their European rulers their real values to them. This has given to Indians especially a renewed determination to secure from England *quid pro quo* in the form of greater political liberty and social privileges. While this has been especially emphasized by Moslems and Indians, it has affected the Christians with so great a spirit of nationalism that the recent All-India Christian Council sent a deputation to the Viceroy requesting the Government to recognize the 3,876,203 Christians of the 1911 census as a community deserving political representation in the Imperial Legislative Council. The increasing demand of all Indians for greater freedom led Parliament to send out a Commission to investigate the situation; and while their report at time of writing has not been published in full, the people of that Empire are assured of many alleviations of existing disabilities. The independent Powers of the Far East also will be benefited in many ways through their coöperation in the war. A greatly feared backset to the cause of missions in China, through the exposure to fierce temptations and from the harsh treatment unavoidable in war of its labor contingent in France, has been met in part by sending to those camps many successful missionaries from North China, as well as a delegation of Christian Chinese studying in American institutions. In Mesopotamia, also, similar work undertaken by Indian missionaries will do much to lessen the ill effects of the war.

Another resultant of the unprecedented conflict comes from the ethical and religious reactions occasioned by seas of Christian blood. An old convert in India pathetically asked his pastor if the great fire in the West were still burning, and a South Sea islander stood bewildered and shaken when he learned that the war was primarily between Christian nations. Keen Japanese were at first ready to declare Christianity a failure because of this stupendous crime of Christendom; but their maturer thought and the increasing barbarity in German initiative has convinced them that instead of its proving the bankruptcy of Christianity, to quote Secretary Oldham, "the War has shown the bankruptcy of a society which has refused to accept and apply the principles of Christianity in social, national and international affairs. As has been well said, 'Christianity has not been tried and found wanting; it has been found difficult and never tried.' "[8] So contrary is it to Christian teachings that for a time the churches in one district in China set apart a day each week for special prayer that this demoniacal evil might be divinely conquered.

But it is more than a problem of Christianity. The Moslem world has been fighting against itself. The Jihad, declared by the Sheikh-ul-Islam and the Sultan of Turkey most solemnly in November, 1915, failed to call to arms a body of fifty millions of fanatical Mohammedans, as had been fervently hoped would be the case. "There was no shock, since there was no sympathetic response. Protests were made by the Moslems of Turkey, while the eighty millions under British control proclaimed their unshaken loyalty; and from Persia, Morocco, Egypt, India, Russia, Algeria and other Moslem countries, Turkey was taken severely to task for forming an alliance with two Christian Powers in a conflict with other Christian nations. . . . Mohammedans are in despair especially since, as a last fatal blow, the Arabs have arisen in open rebellion against Turkey, seizing the sacred places of Islam, and repudiating the right to the office of caliph or of the sultan of Turkey."[9] Similarly an Arabic periodical published

[8] J. H. Oldham, "The World and the Gospel," p. 200.

[9] J. L. Barton in *Missionary Ammunition, Number One,* 1916, p. 19.

in Zanzibar says: "The pillars of the East are tottering, its thrones are being destroyed, its power is being shattered and its supremacy is being obliterated. The Moslem world is divided against itself."[10]

But what have been the effects of this war upon the home base of missions? The financial drafts made by the governments and voluntary organizations of warring nations upon their peoples and the increased cost of everything have affected the treasuries of some of the smaller societies unfavorably. For the most part, however, the mission boards have not only met their expenses but in many cases receipts have been larger than ever before. The contributions thus given have called attention to missions as being both worthy and indispensable elements in the world situation, and hence necessitating their support. Perhaps this is felt most generally among friends of British missions.

Man power causes the societies greater difficulty. Practically the entire German force has been sent from India, or else interned, and to fill their places has made new demands upon other nationalities. The depleted ranks of French societies have not been filled. Great Britain needs all her men for the trenches and has been sorely pressed in trying to supply the foreign fields with the workers absolutely required. Even the United States, since her entry into the war, is experiencing difficulty in keeping missionary candidates from going to the front in Europe instead of reenforcing the thin Asiatic and African battle lines. Hope for improvement in this recruiting is slight, since the call to arms has laid strongest hold upon college and university men. Thus in 1915, out of 52,000 students in German universities, 41,000 were under arms; in France all students except those physically unfit were called out; in Great Britain and Ireland about 50 per cent of the male students were in the army or navy, in Canada 40 per cent, and in Australia 30 per cent.[11] In the United States volunteering

[10] *Missionary Review of the World,* January, 1917, p. 4.

[11] *International Review of Missions,* April, 1916, p. 183.

and the draft have emptied the colleges and universities of practically all the choicest men of twenty-one and upward. If this continues long, an interim must ensue before another college generation furnishes a sufficient number of missionary candidates. Yet it may be expected that the present devotion to a cause that ends so commonly in death or lifelong crippling will end forever the old excuse urged against missionary enlistment, that the service is a hard one and often fatal, in certain unheathful countries. Men will join the colors of the Prince of Peace and of Life even more willingly than they now march under the banners of destruction and death in the hope of establishing once more justice, righteousness and lasting freedom in the earth.

A happy effect of the present stress is found in the growing *rapprochement* between the missions of a given national group, and to a less extent between those of different nations. This is due to the necessity for coöperation in order to make a reduced force serve for the needs of an increasing work. In a few cases already a desire to economize resources has led to readjustment of fields; in others to a temporary filling of vacant places by missionaries of a different denomination or nationality. The home constituencies are thus being taught the beautiful lesson of the trenches as related to true brotherhood and essential Christianity. Perhaps one of the best discussions of this war as affecting the international and interconfessional relationships of missions is that of Dr. J. Schmidlin, a Roman Catholic professor of theology in the University of Münster, found in *The Constructive Quarterly* for December, 1915, from which we quote two sentences: "Thus that which has served to separate missionaries who were comrades in belief and confession—national solidarity and love of country—has also united and reconciled children of the same country who were separated in their belief. Surmounting all barriers of dogma and church polity, men have learned to love and cherish one another, yes, even to recognize that in spite of all that separates us there is much also that binds us together."

Turning now from the effect of the war upon missions, a few paragraphs may be devoted to considering post-bellum reconstruction in mission lands. The Germans, even more than the Allies, are diligently studying the many problems and possibilities of changes necessitated by the readjustments that must surely come. The economic waste of the past four years is almost inconceivably great; and to restore this waste puts upon every nation an amount of production vastly greater than any known in the past. Raw material, freedom of the seas that the manufacturing countries may buy from every land and carry back for sale and distribution the manufactured products, a new enlistment of labor in countries where climate and primitive living make work irksome and unnecessary, an uplift in desires and ideals that new markets may be created, increasing intelligence and friendliness so that coöperation may be willing and profitable—these are some of the essentials of progress after the war.

In earlier cognate discussions, men like Captain Mahan have emphasized the importance of eastward and westward movements in the temperate zone, while others of Benjamin Kidd's school have insisted no less strongly upon the importance of the Tropics and the consequent north and south line of industrial life. A score of years ago nearly, Professor Reinsch, in his "World Politics," startled many American readers by his insistence upon the importance of the undeveloped and unoccupied tropical regions of the globe, mainly in South America and Africa. Even more insistently Kidd's "Control of the Tropics" had, two years before, magnified the same zone, but more particularly the densely peopled tracts with their varied possibilities of production and exploitation. In a recent article by J. A. R. Marriott, M.P., entitled "Welt-Politik," General Smuts of Africa is thus quoted: "Formerly we did not fully appreciate the Tropics as in the economy of civilization. It is only quite recently that people have come to realize that without an abundance of raw material which the Tropics alone can supply, the highly developed industries of today would be impossible. Vegetable and mineral oils, cotton, sisal, rubber, jute and similar products in vast quantities are essential for the industrial world."[12]

Another aspect of tropical Africa is brought out in an article by Herr Emil Zimmerman, writing in the *Europäische Staats und Wirtschaft Zeitung* of June 23, 1917: "If the Great War makes Central Africa German, fifty years hence 500,000 and more Germans can be living there by the side of 50,000,000 blacks. Then there may be an army of 1,000,000 men in German Africa, and the colony will have its own war navy, like Brazil. An England that is strong in Africa dominates the situation in Southern Europe and does not heed us. But from Central Africa we shall dominate the English connections with South Africa, India and Australia, and we shall force English policy to reckon with us."[13] And again Dr. Solf, the German Secretary for Colonies, has lately proposed a simple solution of Africa's industrial future. "In redividing Africa those nations which have proved most humane toward the natives must be favored. Germany has always considered that to colonize meant doing mission work. That is why in the present War the natives of our colonies stick to us. England's colonial history, on the other hand, is nothing but a list of dark crimes."[14] The principle enunciated in the first sentence of this statement is as important and true as the later ones are incorrect, if the present writer's inquiries and observations in British and German East Africa in 1912 are indicative of the facts in the case.

The political problems of the countries here considered are quite as important and perplexing as is their economic status. Three theories of control have been tried: (1) That of plantations or possessions, worked for the possessor's profit with little regard for the governed; (2) the policy of vigorous expansion by the

12 *Nineteenth Century and After*, April, 1918, pp. 675-676.
13 Reported in the London *Times*, November 9, 1917.
14 *Nineteenth Century and After*, April, 1918, p. 681.

whites themselves, despite the perils of tropical environments; and (3) permitting the natives to work out their own development independently, with or without white oversight. Of these the third is the only one favored by the ethics and political sagacity of enlightened nations today. But this demands the consent and good will of the governed, and how may these essentials be secured?

India is the most important, politically considered, of all tropical lands. And that Empire's relation to England the eminent Indian ruler, Sir Herbert Edwardes, declared in an address delivered at Liverpool in 1860, should be that of a stewardship in Christian hands, a designation echoed in Kidd's general phrase, "a trust of civilization," and John H. Harris's "trusteeship *vs.* possession." How shall this trust be fulfilled? Certainly one must consider the question of India's poet laureate, Sir Rabindranath Tagore, "Is the instinct of the West right where she builds her national welfare behind the barricade of a universal distrust of humanity?"[15] Such distrust is not removed by the Indian educational scheme alone, or with the addition of civilization. "If we pursue the *ignis fatuus* of secular education in a pagan land, destitute of other light," quoting Sir Herbert again, "then we English will lose India without those Indians gaining any future."[16] In a similar vein Sir Alfred Lyall testified: "The wildest, as well as the shallowest notion of all, seems to me that universally prevalent belief that education, civilization and increased material prosperity will reconcile the people of India eventually to our rule."[17]

A partial solution of India's political problems is found in the deputation to that Empire in accordance with Mr. Montagu's speech in the House of Commons of August 30, 1917, in the course of which he said: "The policy of His Majesty's Government, with

[15] R. Tagore, "Nationalism," p. 101.

[16] Quoted in W. Archer's "India and Its Future," pp. 307-308.

[17] M. Durand, "Life of Sir Alfred Comyn Lyall," p. 89.

which the Government of India is in complete accord, is that of the increasing association of Indians in every branch of the administration, and the gradual development of self-governing institutions, with a view to the progressive realization of responsible government in India as an integral part of the Indian Empire."[18] The favorable outcome of the deputation's visit has been mentioned already.

Religious problems and readjustments will also be part of the aftermath of the war. At least six millions of Jews, who rightly or wrongly are the objects of the Christian missionary propaganda, have been released from disabilities in Europe, and new careers and educational opportunities will lie before that remarkable race. "Jewish influence in the life of the world, already great in proportion to the size of the community, will gain a fresh accession of strength. Religiously the emancipation may be expected to result, as it has done in other countries, in a decay of Jewish orthodoxy, of which the Jews of the Ghetto have been the main support. While the weakening of the forces of conservatism will open new doors of opportunity to the Christian Church, there is on the other hand the grave danger that many Jews may drift into irreligion and cast the weight of their natural ability and energy on the side of materialism."[19] Mr. Balfour's letter to Lord Rothschild of November 2, 1917, stated that the British Government viewed with favor the establishment in Palestine of a national home for the Jewish people. In the case of missions to Moslem lands, if the Allies are victorious, the work in Turkey will be greatly simplified. Whether this will be the case in Africa depends upon whether the dominant Powers permit missionary organizations to act with greater freedom than they have been granted in the past in North Africa and in certain British possessions. In any case Islam will present strong claims and serious problems for consideration by missionary organizations.

18 *International Review of Missions,* January, 1918, p. 23.

19 *Ibid.*, p. 53.

Is the foreign missionary enterprise willing and competent to aid in the reconstruction soon to come in mission lands? Here are a few typical and representative replies to this important question.

Representing in a semi-official way the missionary societies of the United States and Canada, Dr. Robert E. Speer writes thus: "Foreign Missions are the direct antithesis of the world conditions which men most deplore and the purest expression of the principles which underlie the world order for which men are longing. Foreign Missions represent international friendship and good will. The missionary goes out to help and serve. He bridges the gulf between his own nation and the nation to which he goes. He is not seeking to exploit, or to take advantage, or to make gain. He is seeking only to befriend and aid. And his aim and spirit are internationally unifying. The missionaries succeed in surmounting all the hindrances of nationality and language in binding different peoples together in good will. Furthermore, they are demonstrating the possibility of the existence of a strong nationalistic spirit side by side with human brotherhood and international unity. They are seeking to develop in each nation a national church embodying and inspiring and consecrating to God the genius and destiny of each nation. But they are doing this because these are the elements of a yet larger unity, the unity of mankind. The first is not contradictory to the second; it is essential to it, as the perfection of the State requires the perfection of the family unit, and the family demands and does not exclude the richest individualism. It is out of her perfect ministry to the life of each nation that the Church is to be prepared to minister to the life of all humanity and to achieve its unity."[20]

As editor of *The International Review of Missions* and secretary of the Edinburgh Continuation Committee, Mr. J. H. Oldham states his views of the world-functions of missions: "Missions are the antithesis of war. They have created between different

[20] *Missionary Ammunition, Number One,* 1916, pp. 12-13.

peoples relations, not of competition, but of coöperation. With all their shortcomings they are an embodiment of the idea that the stronger and more advanced nations exist to uplift the weaker and more backward. They are a vital expression of the principle on which the new society must rest. . . . The gospel of love must embody itself in act no less manifestly than selfishness and brutality have expressed themselves in the terrible scenes that the world has witnessed. The non-Christian races fear, not without cause, that the object of western peoples is to exploit them. Missions must convince them that the Church exists to help and serve them, and the desire to serve them must be made evident in ways that they can understand. The task of Missions thus grows broader and larger than we at first conceived."[21]

And such statements are not the claims of interested propagandists merely,—officials employed by missionary organizations, and hence liable to overrate the character and importance of missions to the nations. Few men have traversed the world as extensively and observantly as Sir Harry Johnston, and probably no one equals him in his varied administrative and anthropological services to Africa. In his Introduction to the Cambridge University Maitland Prize Essay for 1915, he says: "Although the writer . . . is so heterodox a professor of Christianity, practical experience in Africa, Asia and America has brought home to him ever and again during the last thirty-four years the splendid work which has been and is being accomplished by all types of Christian missionary amongst the Black, Brown and Yellow peoples of non-Caucasian race, and amid those Mediterranean or Asiatic Caucasians whose skins may be a little duskier than ours, but whose far-back ancestry was the same, whose minds and bodies are of our type, but whose mentality has been dwarfed and diverted from the amazing development of the European by false faiths,—false in their interpretation of Cosmos, false to the best human ideals in daily life."

21 *International Review of Missions,* October, 1914, pp. 632-633.

On a later page he upholds with the author "the work of Christian missionaries in general and lays down the rule that our relations with the backward peoples of the world should be carried on consonantly with the principles of Christian ethics—pity, patience, fair-mindedness, protection and instruction; with a view not to making them the carefully guarded serfs of the White race, but to enable them some day to be entirely self-dependent, and yet interdependent with us on universal human coöperation in world management."

And once more this British administrator asserts: "The value of the Christian missionary is that he serves no government. He is not the agent of any selfish State, or self-seeking community. He does not even follow very closely the narrow-minded limitations of the Church or the sect that has sent him on his mission. He is the servant of an Ideal, which he identifies with God; and this ideal is in its essence not distinguishable from essential Christianity; which is at one and the same time essential common sense, real liberty, a real seeking after progress and betterment. He preaches chastity and temperance, the obeying of such laws as are made by the community; but consonantly with all constitutional and peaceful efforts, he urges the bringing of man-made laws more and more into conformity with Christian principles."[22]

As representing nations of ancient culture coming under the helpful influences of Christian missions, perhaps no one will command a more attentive hearing than Marquis Okuma, ex-premier of Japan and one of the world's foremost statesmen. From a summary of his address, delivered at the semi-centennial of Protestant missions in that Empire, we excerpt the following: "The coming of missionaries to Japan was the means of linking this country to the Anglo-Saxon spirit to which the heart of Japan has always responded. The success of Christian work in Japan can be measured by the extent to which it has been able

[22] A. J. Macdonald, "Trade, Politics and Christianity in Africa and the East," xii, xv, xviii.

to infuse the Anglo-Saxon and the Christian spirit into the nation. It has been a means of putting into these fifty years an advance equivalent to that of a hundred years. Japan has a history of 2,500 years, and 1,500 years ago had advanced in civilization and domestic arts, but never took wide views, nor entered upon wide work. Only by the coming of the West in its missionary representatives, and by the spread of the Gospel, did the nation enter upon world-wide thoughts and world-wide work. This is a great result of the Christian spirit. To be sure Japan had her religions, and Buddhism prospered greatly; but this prosperity was largely through political means. Now this creed [Buddhism] has been practically rejected by the better classes who, being spiritually thirsty, have nothing to drink."[23]

These representative testimonies suggest both the fitness and the willingness of Christian missions to participate in the coming international readjustments necessitated by the war. Such an enterprise supplies what the war-weary world so greatly needs—the *élan vital et créatur*, to borrow Bergson's fine phrase. And the missionary leaders are alert and at their task. On April 4, 1918, Drs. John R. Mott and Charles R. Watson, representing the missionary boards of the United States and Canada, met with the Standing Committee of Missionary Societies in Great Britain and Ireland, when it was resolved to form an international "Emergency Committee of Coöperating Missions." Already the British committee had been consulted by the Government concerning certain important matters affecting the mission fields and their problems arising from the war. Such questions are becoming increasingly numerous, and their solution demands an intimate knowledge of missions and of the spirit and aspirations of African and Asiatic races. America is likewise needing such a body of experts to supplement government investigations. This country has a slight preponderance in representation on the Emergency Committee; and in the chairman, Dr. John R. Mott, the foremost

[23] *Japan Daily Mail*, October 9, 1909.

Protestant leader of the world, and a man of such diplomatic gifts that President Wilson twice vainly called him to the position of minister to China,—though he accepted appointment upon commissions to deal with Mexico and Russia later,—the committee has a missionary statesman who is equal to the important trusts that will be committed to its consideration. To serve as the eyes, ears and hands of this important post-bellum council, the two largest fields, India and China, have each an energetic Continuation Committee of the Edinburgh Conference of 1910, established as the result of Dr. Mott's visits and conferences in 1912-1913. The Foreign Missions Conference of North America, and especially its Board of Reference and Counsel, are in annual and *ad interim* consultation as questions arise from time to time.

President King quotes these words from Lloyd George's address to a labor delegation: "Don't always be thinking of getting back where we were before the War. Get a really new world. I firmly believe that what is known as the after-the-War settlement will direct the destinies of all classes for generations to come. I believe the settlement after the War will succeed in proportion to its audacity. The readier we are to cut away from the past, the better we are likely to succeed. Think out new ways, new methods, of dealing with old problems."[24]

Another horizon of the same idealistic character opens before the eyes of our own President, the seer to the nations in this epoch-making time. In an address delivered on October 5, 1916, President Wilson proclaims the new day to the United States: "America up to the present time has been, as if by deliberate choice, confined and provincial, and it will be impossible for her to remain confined and provincial. Henceforth she belongs to the world and must act as part of the world, and all the attitudes of America will henceforth be altered." And again three weeks later he adds: "America was established in order to indicate, at any rate in one government, the fundamental rights of man.

[24] F. Lynch, "President Wilson and the Moral Aims of the War," p. 72.

America must hereafter be ready as a member of the family of nations to exert her whole force, moral and physical, to the assertion of those rights throughout the round world." Here is a sentence from his greetings to France on Bastille Day, 1918: "The War is being fought to save ourselves from intolerable things; but it is also being fought to save mankind." And as a final word from President Wilson, taken from his discussion of the new international morality: "My urgent advice to you would be, not always to think first of America, but always, also, to think first of humanity. You do not love humanity, if you seek to divide humanity into jealous camps. Humanity can be welded together only by love, by sympathy, by justice, not by jealousy and hatred." While none of these utterances refer specifically to missions, yet surely Dr. W. I. Hull is correct in interpreting President Wilson's relation to races of the mission fields in these words: "Instead of exploiting backward peoples, he would apply the maxim of *noblesse oblige*, and would summon all nations to mutual aid in their ascent of 'the world's great altar stairs' up to the law and order, peace and justice, which constitute the true sunshine of God."[25]

The "really new world" of Britain's Premier will not be dominated by Machiavelli, the motto of whose sixteenth and seventeenth century monarchs was "*L'état c'est moi!*" even though Treitschke ranked him second only to Aristotle as a political philosopher.[26] The present cataclysm of woes does not prove Professor Cramb's contention that "Corsica has conquered Galilee"; nor has Nietzsche thrust the "pale Galilean" from his throne. That semi-insane philosopher's *Uebermenschen* must fall before Sir John Macdonnell's "*Super-Nationalism*" as set forth in the March, 1918, issue of the *Contemporary Review*. And the President's world-echoed phrase, "world-democracy," is uttered only with the corrective in mind that was sounded forth a score

25 F. Lynch, "President Wilson and the Moral Aims of the War," p. 64.

26 H. von Treitschke, "Politik," p. 3.

of years ago by England's Colonial Secretary, Joseph Chamberlain, "Think imperially." It is only by the establishment of an *Imperium in imperio* through obedience to what the Duke of Wellington called the Christian's Marching Orders, the Great Commission, that the new reign of the Prince of Peace can become possible. If the blood-soaked "savagery of civilization on the march to save the world from the civilization of savagery" is the dolorous duty of the present hour, there is solace in the thought that Golgotha was but the prelude to the Resurrection and Ascension. The Ascent of Mankind in all its nations and peoples and kindreds and tongues is at hand. To hasten this universal uplift and aid the World Powers as they seek to inaugurate the New Order, no agency is likely to aid more than foreign missions among the peoples reached by that enterprise. And the new Imperial Thinking and Acts are simply those of the seven-fold Commission of the Saviour of the World, "Behold, pray, go, heal, preach, teach, baptize, all nations," the conquering Labarum of an onward-moving Church.

VIII

THE WAR AND SOCIAL WORK

WILLIAM BACON BAILEY

ALTHOUGH the duration of this world-war, and the part which we may be called upon to play in it, makes the destruction in wealth and human life in this country uncertain, and although we cannot tell so far in advance what will be the probable extent of social reconstruction to follow, still the war has progressed far enough, and its effects upon this country are sufficiently apparent, to enable us to forecast more or less indefinitely certain changes which are likely to follow its close.

With regard to the future of social service, three facts are apparent:

First, the people of our country are contributing money as never before to social work. We have for a long time realized that there was a reservoir in this country upon which we had drawn but little, but few realized the extent of this surplus. At times of great distress both here and abroad, our sympathy had been expressed by generous contributions. We had annually contributed large sums for the support of various philanthropies in this country, but as a nation we never realized how much we could give until the test came. One drive is hardly completed before another comes. We are surprised as a nation and as individuals at the amounts we can repeatedly give and still continue to meet our ordinary expenditures. This giving is getting to be almost a habit with us and when the war is over, although we may be helping to carry a huge national debt, I believe that our deserving charities will be supported more adequately than before the war.

Second, we are getting more trained volunteer workers. One of the principal problems of charitable organizations engaged in case work has been to secure a sufficient number of capable volunteers who would keep their interest in the work and be regular in their attendance. The past few months have seen an increase in this volunteer service which a year ago we should never have deemed possible. The Home Service Section of the American Red Cross has enlisted the service as visitors of thousands of our men and women who are anxious to do what they can to preserve the homes from which some member has been called to the colors. In a large number of cities this service has been placed under the supervision of paid workers who had been connected with charity organization societies and who brought with them the experience of years in directing and training volunteer friendly visitors. They recognized the advantage of classroom instruction for these visitors, even if necessity compelled that it be extremely limited. Accordingly training schools for these volunteers have been started in many places in this country and the attendance has been surprisingly large and regular. These volunteers are no longer timidly inquiring whether there is some opportunity for friendly visiting in the homes; they are demanding that some opportunity be given them. After the war this vast army of workers with limited training will demand work of a similar nature and the problem of finding satisfactory volunteers should be solved for many years to come.

Third, the war is raising the standard of care in charitable work. Most of these volunteers are visiting in soldiers' families. The allowance from the Government, the State and the Red Cross makes possible a good standard of living. While our soldiers are at the front they do not need to fear that the standard to which the family had been accustomed will be allowed to fall. At the close of hostilities these volunteers, accustomed to this standard, will demand that the same standard apply to the out-door relief given by charitable societies. The result will be a considerable rise in the standard of care. Professional social workers are not talking so much as they did about "cases." They are talking more about "families." This is the express desire of those who are directing the Home Service Section of the Red Cross. It is felt that in this way a more personal note may be brought into family rehabilitation in the future. It would appear, therefore, that the future should find our charities more adequately financed, better supplied with trained volunteers, and inspired to a higher standard of work.

The habit of saving is likely to become much more firmly established among our people. We may never be so thrifty as the French nation, but we are progressing in that direction. Subscriptions to the Third Liberty Loan were received from seventeen millions of our people. In many of our public schools the purchase of thrift stamps by the scholars has been almost universal. It is probable that a very large proportion of those who are now purchasing liberty bonds never owned a bond of any description before. The habit formed in this way will continue in many cases. A banker a short time ago prophesied that upon the conclusion of this war the savings banks would receive far larger deposits than had ever been the case before. This habit of saving and the ownership of bonds will not fail to have its influence upon the rank and file of our people. At the close of the war we shall have our troubles with those who will advance repudiation or some scheme by which the burden of our national debt may be shifted and the necessity for saving miraculously avoided in some way. But the common sense of our people will assert itself and we shall realize that the only way by which we can replace this capital is by spending less than we earn. The plain word "thrift" seems likely to come into its own again.

Up to the present time social work has appeared to many persons to be a fad. Some have felt that people with too little to do have spent their time in interfering with the affairs of people who had too much to do. The charge has been made that social service was only a temporary phenomenon which would soon disappear. But the war has taught us a lesson. The military authorities were among the first to recognize the need of proper recreation for the troops, and the demand for workers in the cantonments and at the front has been too great to be met. We see now that the need for recreation is a real need. It seems likely that commercialized recreation and amusement is likely to play a smaller part hereafter, and that the community is going to demand a share in this enterprise in the future. Assembly halls, playgrounds, and similar provisions for the public will be required.

We have never had a caste system in this country and aristocracy based upon birth has been unknown. It is probable that nowhere in the world during the past two centuries has it been easier for a man to improve his financial and social standing by his own efforts than in this country. Land ownership has been widely distributed, we have had a large middle class and men have been constantly changing from the group of employees to that of employers. But notwithstanding these factors, there has been a growth of class feeling in this country. Employers have been mistrusted by employees. The growth of large fortunes has given rise to envy and bitterness in many quarters. Many have felt that ignorance was the principal cause for this growing antipathy. Employer and employee no longer met upon a common footing. Many attempts have been made to bridge this chasm. Settlement houses have been erected in order that individuals who would not be likely to meet in the usual course of business or social intercourse might here become acquainted and learn one another's viewpoint. The industrial service movement has been an attempt to link the interests of employer and employee together. But these movements have only scratched the surface. The distinctions based on difference have persisted. It has remained for the war to bring the members of these opposing groups together. Camp and trench life know no class distinction. Rich and poor, educated and illiterate, rub elbows and share common life. It is no uncommon sight to find four men with three different mother tongues sharing a tent together. The effect of this close companionship, this sharing of dangers in common, cannot help but breed a companionship which will do much to bring together men of different birth, breeding and social station.

Another effect of this war has been to lessen sectarian and religious differences. Protestant, Roman Catholic and Jewish organizations are working side by side in our military camps. The contributions to the work of the Knights of Columbus and of the Y. M. C. A. have come from the community as a whole. Men of different faiths have served as members of the same teams in these drives. The lessons learned in this way are not likely to be forgotten and the great charities to survive this war will probably draw their support from a wider public regardless of sectarian affiliation.

We often heard at the beginning of this conflict that it was a rich man's war; that this country had been drawn into it through the machinations of wealthy men who wished to make more wealth through army contracts. This charge has been pretty thoroughly disproven, and now little is heard of it. The rich have proved their patriotism as conclusively as any class in this country. They have contributed generously to our war charities, have submitted to unprecedented taxation with very little grumbling, have bought Liberty Bonds generously, and have seen their sons volunteer for military service with commendable pride. Many of our most efficient executives have contributed their time to the service of the Government. In fact, one of the most interesting and inspiring features of this war has been the service rendered by our men and women of wealth and social position.

The war is also likely to change the extent and direction of the social movements in this country. In the early days most of the charitable work in this country was directed to the amelioration of the condition of some particular group of unfortunates. A group of their compatriots in this country would form a society for the assistance of Scotch widows. No study was made of the causes of this unfortunate situation. The widows were there and their helpless condition called for aid. There was no attempt to reduce the number of widows by safeguarding the lives of their husbands. In this assistance there was much duplication as the number of these societies increased. Then came the attempt to eliminate this waste by the formation of societies to coördinate these charitable activities in our cities. Although the idea of constructive work entered the minds of these pioneers, the contributors were interested chiefly in the relief of want.

It soon became evident that this want was the result of certain well-defined causes. Sickness, unemployment, intemperance and child labor were recognized as the causes of misery and the extent of these causes was studied by societies which worked for their removal. These activities soon brought the realization that many of these causes were social rather than individual. Sickness is sometimes caused by individual excesses, but it is also caused by unhealthful occupations and life in miserable tenements. We had held property rights as sacred, but when greed brought a train of social evils we directed our attention to regulation. It may be meritorious to help a widow whose husband has been killed at a machine, but it is equally meritorious to safeguard the machine that it may cease to be the cause of widowhood in the future. It is good philanthropy to assist those afflicted with tuberculosis, but it is better to remove the disease-breeding "lung blocks" from our communities.

This brought the realization that these are community problems which must be met by community action. The state legislatures were appealed to with ever increasing success, but Federal action was difficult to obtain. The war has made us impatient with half-measures. The exigency demanded immediate and drastic action. Things have been done to obtain efficiency which we would have considered impossible five years ago. The rights of private property have had to give way before community need. We have begun to deal on a larger scale with ultimate causes and less with the relief of apparent effects. This movement may receive a temporary setback at the close of the war, but as a community we have learned what is possible and this lesson will not be lost.

Certain social reforms are being hastened by the war. We have long felt that certain practices were harmful or wasteful, but in our easy-going manner had kept putting the matter off in the hope that the evil would cure itself. The necessity of waging successful war has compelled the immediate elimination of this waste. Take one or two instances only.

For a long time we have been more or less familiar with the financial, physical and spiritual waste resulting from the consumption of intoxicants in this country. We have been interested in this problem for a half century and various attempts have been made to eliminate the most serious evils connected with excessive drinking without interfering with a moderate use of alcohol. Our half-hearted attempts were not very successful and finally, after we had experienced a coal shortage, and had accepted wheatless and meatless days, the country at last made up its mind that intoxicants must go and the liquor traffic in this country appears to be doomed. It might have come sooner or later in any case, but the war has hastened the day.

For a long time penologists have realized that it was poor economy to shut prisoners into dark and dismal cells, giving them but scant exercise with little or no employment and then to expect them, at the expiration of their terms, to be returned ready to take their proper places in society. We have realized that outdoor labor on farms was one of the best things for this class because in this way the prisoners could be built up in health and be made more or less self-supporting while serving their terms. But we had the jails on hand and it was perhaps the easiest plan to lock the prisoners in their cells with the assurance that they could be found when wanted. The demand for farm labor has finally forced our jails and penitentiaries to give up the labor so sorely needed on the farms. It is probable that during the coming summer a million acres of land in this country will be tilled by those undergoing sentence.

We had recognized for years the ravages of venereal disease upon our manhood and womanhood, and a national society and a large number of state societies had been organized to combat the evil. But when the figures began to be published showing the incidence of these diseases among our troops the public awoke to the seriousness of the situation. The Federal Government has taken steps to remove diseased women from the neighborhood of the army cantonments and naval bases. The Government is footing the bills for the treatment of these women in state institutions, where such exist, and is providing suitable facilities for their care in the states where no such opportunity for treatment existed. After the war the lesson we have learned in this way is not likely to be forgotten. Another lesson we have learned from the war has been that a considerable proportion of our young men are physically below par. Poor care of the teeth and body, improper or insufficient food, lack of proper exercise, unhygienic methods of living, and various forms of excesses have produced a generation of young men many of whom are physically unfit for active military service. The importance of this fact has now been driven home, and although much had been said and written upon this subject in recent years, it will have added emphasis in the future.

We have always had a democratic form of government, and have in a way considered this country an asylum for the oppressed of all nations. For several years previous to the outbreak of the war in Europe, we had been receiving into this country immigrants at the rate of about a million a year. We had gradually increased the number of restrictions until most of the undesirable types were excluded. We had made the process of naturalization comparatively easy and had left it to the individual immigrant to decide whether or not he would become a citizen. We had recognized the desirability of Americanizing these immigrants as soon as possible, but had proceeded about the proposition in a more or less half-hearted way. The Y. M. C. A., through its industrial department, and through the industrial service work in connection with the colleges, had done considerable to teach English and civics to the non-English-speaking foreigners. Several other organizations, some of them national in scope, had interested themselves in this problem, but our country seemed slow to appreciate the necessity of making true Americans from these various racial groups at the earliest possible moment. The war has brought home to us the fact that we have alien enemies in our midst and from this time we may expect to make a much more thoroughgoing attempt to Americanize these groups. The National Council of Defense is investigating this question at present and we may with confidence look to a well-considered plan of campaign from this body.

The very fact that we were receiving from the Old World annually a gift of a million foreign-born, most of whom were in the active ages, has led us to think that the supply of labor for this country was assured. We were receiving from Europe all of the natural increase from a population half as large as our own. The ships that brought these hopeful workers to this country took back many who had been maimed in our industries. We had paid too little attention to this problem since the source of this supply of cheap labor seemed inexhaustible. Upon the declaration of hostilities in Europe, the stream of labor to this country suddenly ceased and it is a serious question whether it will ever again reach its former proportion. Most of the European countries are going to be so drained of their young men that a large emigration from them is not to be expected for a long time to come. The demands for raw material and finished products from certain of the European countries has increased tremendously and a shortage of labor in this country has been the result. Concerns have bid against one another to secure sufficient labor and for the first time in years we have a condition in which the demand for labor of all kinds exceeds the supply. With the impossibility of securing this needed labor from abroad, we have realized the necessity of conserving the supply in this country. Every effort must be made to reduce the toll from accident and injury and to decrease the amount of sickness in the country. We may expect an increase in compensation insurance and in health insurance among the states. This summer we are having a campaign to save the lives of a hundred thousand children. This movement for the conservation of life would undoubtedly have come in time but has been hastened by the war. Thousands of our young men will be returned to us from overseas more or less crippled and steps are already being taken to give them expert training to fit them for some useful occupation. It is only a step to provide the same sort of training for those who are maimed in our industries.

No matter what may be the waste in life and property resulting from such a conflict, if the people of this country can preserve in their purity the ideals with which they have entered upon this crusade, social workers may face the future with confidence.

IX

THE WAR AND CHURCH UNITY

WILLISTON WALKER

THE great war has been conspicuously one of alliances. For its successful accomplishment coöperation and individual subordination have been manifested in military, political and economic fields in heretofore unexampled fulness. Liberties, the result of long struggles, and deeply cherished, have been laid aside, for the time, that larger efficiency may be accomplished. Individual opinions strongly held have been subordinated to a common purpose. The time has witnessed a reappreciation of values in many realms. Much that in days of peace has seemed of importance, has appeared in the fierce light of war of relatively minor significance. A change of perspective has been the consequence. Has this result, so apparent in most realms of activity and of ordinary life, been manifest in the realm of religion? Are the same forces at work there also? An answer to these questions cannot as yet be fully formulated; but it is at least possible to indicate certain influences which are at work.

The entry of the United States into the world-war has been in a degree unexampled in the history of this country a response to the appeal of righteousness. No action in which the nation has ever engaged has been so unselfish. We have taken our part in the struggle without hate, and with full consciousness of the prospective cost in life and treasure, that certain principles of justice may prevail, and that despotism, brutality and falsehood may not dominate the civilized world. We look for no indemnities, no annexations, and no pecuniary rewards. The American people has never more fully exhibited that idealism which, in spite of frequent misapprehension by those unacquainted with the real national spirit, is its fundamental characteristic. The consonance of this attitude with some primary teachings of religion is apparent. Self-sacrifice that the weak may be helped, that wrong may be resisted, and that a truer and juster order may be established among the nations, are aims that are closely akin to those of the Christian faith in its aspect of love to one's neighbor. Nor is it without evidential value to the essentially religious quality of American life that no enterprise has ever so united the people, and that Americans, whether so by long inheritance or immigrants who have more recently caught the national spirit, have never before been so at one in a common endeavor. Nothing less noble, less idealistic, less in a true sense religious could so have fused them into one.

The war, furthermore, has been a revelation of the fundamental purposefulness of the rising generation. The years immediately antecedent to the struggle saw not a little shaking of older heads over what were called the irresponsibility and pleasure-seeking of our young people. The call to arms has shown them as patriotic, as whole-hearted in devotion, as sacrificial as ever their elders were. They need bow in reverence to none who have gone before them. The cheerfulness with which a selective draft has been accepted, and in thousands of cases anticipated, has shown the readiness of youthful response to high appeal. This demonstration of the soundness, the earnestness and the unselfishness of those who are soon to be the leaders of the national life is full of religious encouragement.

Equally heartening has been the cheerful and effective answer of the responsible population of America to limitations in food and drink that the needs of the Allies should be met and the national resources conserved. Doubtless other nations in the world-struggle have made larger sacrifices and endured far severer privations; but the impressive quality of what America has done is that it has been so largely self-imposed, a voluntary sacrifice, in which suggestion rather than compulsion has been the task of its leaders. Strikingly impressive, also, has been the outpouring of wealth and effort to relieve human suffering through the Red Cross and kindred agencies, not only for the alleviation of the miseries of our own sons, but of the martyred population of Belgium, of France, of Poland and of Syria. No village has been too small, no community too remote or too rural, to have a share in this altruistic endeavor. Its spirit is in a true sense that of religion. More openly and professedly religious has been the marvelous work of the Young Men's Christian Association and of the Knights of Columbus. No previous war has seen anything comparable in extent of effort or scope of plan. The aim, and to a great extent the accomplishment, has been to cast Christian sympathy and brotherly helpfulness around the soldier and sailor in every camp at home and abroad, in the trenches, the hospitals, the battleships, the transports, and in the cities where his furlough is spent and his ideals so easily forgotten. These agencies have not labored for our own sons alone, but for those of France and Italy also. Even more impressive than the vast sums of money contributed from all over the United States for this cause have been the numbers and the quality of the men and women who have given themselves freely and in Christian consecration to this service. The Young Men's Christian Association and the Knights of Columbus have been in truth the right arm of American Christianity stretched out to shelter, to hearten and to aid. They have been the agents of the churches in their ministry. Without them the contribution of organized American Christianity would have been relatively ineffective. Through them that Christianity has exhibited itself in practical and achieving power as never before.

The outstanding feature of these conspicuous manifestations of American religious life is that they have been absolutely undogmatic. Their type of Christianity has been broadly inclusive of what may be called universally accepted doctrine. Chaplains from most various denominational antecedents have labored together in a spirit of Christian comradeship, bearing only the sign of the cross. The workers, ministerial and lay, recruited by the Young Men's Christian Association have been drawn from all shades of American Evangelicalism and have wrought not only harmoniously one with another, but with the Knights of Columbus and with the representatives of Jewish faith. In common efforts to reach common needs, differences which loomed large at home have been laid aside. The requirements and experiences of our soldiers and sailors have been elemental, and these agencies have sought to meet them with a simple, earnest, uncontroversial Gospel,—the common denominator, if it may so be called, of our American Christianity. They have presented God, sin, salvation, faith in Christ, purity of life, brotherly helpfulness; and to this presentation the young manhood of our armies and navies has been quick to respond. These young men have cared little as to the particular denominational label which these messengers may have worn at home. Spoken with manliness, sincerity and sympathy, the message has won their hearts.

These experiences have inevitably raised the question more insistently, which had already before the war been sounded increasingly loudly in our home churches, whether the divided state of American Christianity is to continue. It has long been deplored. Can it not be in a measure abated? A disposition to believe that it can is increasingly evident. The enlarging support given to the Federal Council of the Churches of Christ since the beginning of the war is significant of a growing conviction that at least a larger federal coöperation is not merely desirable but feasible. The much-divided Lutheran body has taken steps which promise its union in one fold. The last General Assembly of the Presbyterian Church of the United States has empowered a committee to issue a call for a Council to meet before the close of the present year by which practical action may be initiated looking towards the organic union of all American Evangelical Christianity. The Protestant Episcopal Church of the United States still urges its ambitious and remote plan of a World Conference on Faith and Order, aiming at a general reunion of Christendom; though in this case the war seems to have delayed rather than furthered the project. In the local field, the scarcity of fuel during the recent winter led to hundreds of instances of temporary combinations of congregations representative of different denominations throughout the northern portion of the United States. Not only has no evil been the consequence, but better acquaintance and larger Christian sympathy have resulted. In some places, as in New Brunswick, N. J., these temporary unions have led to efforts to make these combinations permanent. It is evident that the possibility of a larger unity is being discussed as never before, and in a spirit which more than at any previous time tends to emphasize the great truths in which Christians are agreed and to minimize their differences.

Will anything permanently effective come out of this widely diffused desire? Shall we be satisfied with the remarkable exhibitions of Christian coöperation in our army and navy, shall we entertain a pious wish that something similar may be achieved at home, and will the end of the war find us, nevertheless, in our present divided state? The answer will depend on the sacrificial willingness of our American Christianity. Is it ready to pay the cost? That is a far-reaching question any answer to which is at present impossible, for the difficulties in the path of a larger union are enormous. Such a greater unity can be achieved only as several barriers of great strength are overthrown.

One such barrier is the inertia of local organizations. Few American communities are not confessedly overchurched, as far as the Protestant population is concerned. The spectacle of eight or ten relatively feeble churches ministering to needs which two or three larger bodies could much more effectively meet is one exhibited in hundreds of communities. Yet effective consolidation is opposed by serious obstacles. Long custom, ancient disputes, denominational loyalties, keep these relatively feeble bodies asunder. These prejudices are hard to overcome. "Our fathers worshipped in this mountain," is a feeling not peculiar to Samaria. Much of this local loyalty is not without its commendable qualities. It is bound up with traditions of parental piety, of devotion to a particular house of worship and to a congregation of believers in which one has grown up in the Christian life. These feelings are very real. Yet it is only as the advantages of a larger local unity become evident that our churches can rise to a greater consolidation and more effectively meet the local situation. Only the larger good can drive out the lesser goods.

A further barrier, and one of no inconsiderable magnitude, which renders local union difficult is that our local churches are parts of large organic wholes for the advancement of the Kingdom of God at home and abroad. By their gifts, their sons and daughters and their prayers, the missionary societies are supported, by which the outreaching work of the Kingdom of Christ is carried forward. These societies are now denominational. If two local churches are to become one, where will their joint contributions go? One has aided one group of missionary societies hitherto, the other another. Shall the new union divide its gifts? If it does, will they be as extensive or the interest as great as formerly? These are practical questions for the missionary societies. The only final solution of such a situation would seem to be an extensive consolidation of the missionary societies themselves, so that they might become more representative of American Christianity, at least of American Evangelical Christianity, as a whole, rather than simply the organs of particular denominations.

A third barrier of difficulty barring the pathway of local consolidation is that of ministerial and ecclesiastical responsibility. Each of the various denominations now has its definite method of entrance on its ministry, and of responsibility for the character and standing of those in its pastorates. Each holds itself bound to aid its feebler churches in their pecuniary necessities. If a new congregation results from the union of two or more existing bodies representative of different denominations, where is the test of ministerial fitness, and the guarantee of continued ministerial standing to be found, and who is to aid such a church if financially feeble? These are the problems which are often raised by the so-called "community church." Of course these difficulties are often met by the united organization attaching itself to the denomination originally represented by one of its component parts; but this solution, though effective, makes so large demands on Christian self-denial as often to be impracticable in the present still comparatively feebly developed desire for unity.

A still further barrier to unity, both on the local field and on the larger national scale, is the fact, often overlooked, that the separations of American Christianity are really due quite as much to differences of taste as to divergencies of doctrines or of polity. There is an Episcopal, a Presbyterian or a Methodist way of doing things that really differentiates these great families of believers quite as fully as their more generally acknowledged divergencies. They view the Christian life, they look upon worship, they express their deeper feelings, in unlike ways. The variety is not so much a diversity of belief as a contrast of temperaments. Being so, it is not susceptible to argument, or to adjustment by conventions or creedal agreements. It is to be met, if met at all, by the increasing spirit of democracy, which the war has done so much to foster. In proportion as the fundamental Christian democracy of America becomes a real consciousness these temperamental unlikenesses will tend to be subordinated to a larger unity of spirit. They will continue. Men are not all made in the same mould. But, it may be believed that they may be overcome by a growing recognition of unity in variety.

Moreover, in spite of an increasing longing that the multitudinous subdivisions of American Christianity be merged in a larger whole, much tenacious holding of peculiar denominational tenets will have to be overcome. The simplicity of the great truths which Christians hold in common will need to be more fully realized. Most American Evangelical denominations are now willing freely to admit that the essential verities of Christianity are held by their associated communions, and that a true Christian life is possible in each of them. The evident working of the spirit of God makes a denial impossible. But while each denomination is thus willing to recognize a real, if grudgingly admitted, sisterhood as the share of the others, each regards its peculiarities of belief or practice as of extreme importance, if not to the being, at least to the well-being of the church, so that effective intercommunion seems impossible. An interesting illustration of this spirit has recently been shown in a discussion involving a communion which professes, one cannot doubt with sincerity, a desire for a reunion of Christendom. A proposition was made to it by a number of representatives of other communions, urging that the unity of American Christianity be illustrated by joint ordinations of chaplains for service with the army and navy. That proposal, which involved no question of ministerial status in the home churches, was declined by its highest authorities. It is not conceivable that those who thus refused it believed that chaplains went forth to their arduous task in the name of Christ from other communions without the blessing of God; but such differences of apprehension as may still coexist with obedience to the one Master are evidently yet deemed too great to permit mutual Christian authorization for service. Doubtless many similar instances could be found, but as long as they characterize American Christianity at all they reveal the persistence of a spirit which exalts denominational peculiarities above the full recognition of common Christian discipleship.

These barriers have been thus frankly stated because they are very real, and while the impulse toward Christian unity now flows in increasing strength from the experiences of the great war, the movement in that direction must acquire far greater momentum before its work can be accomplished. Christian unity was never so fully before the thought of the American churches as now. Never were so many sincerely desirous of it. Never was its need so obvious as in these days when the church faces the tremendous problem of the reconstruction on a Christian basis of a shattered social order. It is a task which demands all the forces of an undivided Christianity. Yet desirable as the goal of unity is, it will never be reached save through the strenuous coöperant effort of all who long for it. That effort must be greater than any heretofore made. It must be patient and persistent and in full faith that the Master's prayer for his disciples demands their utmost endeavor.

Three steps are certainly needful for effective progress towards a larger unity:

There must be a clearer recognition of the things in the Christian faith which are of vital significance. The really great truths must be seen in their proper perspective. The simplicity of the Gospel must be increasingly recognized. We have too often elevated relatively subordinate convictions to an equality with the fundamentals of the faith. In this clearer perception of proportions the experiences of the religious work of the war is greatly aiding. We are seeing that in the Christian life we need not so many things as much.

No less necessary is it that a spirit ready to sacrifice the important, but relatively subordinate, be developed. No denomination is called upon to sacrifice alone. If unity is to be achieved, each must feel a willingness to subordinate that which though precious by custom or antiquity or cherished possession is yet divisive.

Even more imperative is it that American religious bodies know each other better. Existing side by side, laboring in the same communities, it is amazing how little real comprehension of each other's spiritual life now exists. In mutual acquaintance by common association, wherever such intercourse can be brought about, lies the corrective of much present misunderstanding that separates us. All that aids a common acquaintance is an aid to ultimate unity.

The consideration just mentioned makes it probable that the most promising present step is in the direction of federal coöperation. Religious bodies that are far from willing to sink their present differences may yet work in harmony, and by working together increase that mutual understanding and thereby confidence in each other's Christian spirit which is so essential a preliminary to unity. That is what makes the Federal Council of the Churches of Christ and similar movements eminently worthy of support. They are not ends in themselves. They are means of utmost significance to a larger end.

The war is showing a vision of our need and of the goal of our effort. That the road to a larger and more effective unity of the religious forces of America is full of difficulties is no reason why a Christian man should hesitate to tread it. It is as true now as when the Master said it, that "with God all things are possible."

X

THE RELIGIOUS BASIS OF WORLD RE-ORGANIZATION[1]

E. HERSHEY SNEATH

WHEN we reflect upon the situation of the race today, with the leading nations in the throes of a war of unparalleled dimensions and destructiveness, we are appalled at the impotency of those forces that heretofore have tended toward world-organization. Time was when international treaties and laws seemed to have at least a semblance of inhibiting sanctity, but in recent years they are regarded in certain quarters as mere "scraps of paper," and the supposed "rights" of nations are treated with scorn and contempt. The black flag of piracy, hitherto regarded as the symbol of international outlawry, floats on the high seas, and the assassination of neutrals and noncombatants is regarded by some as a national virtue. For centuries humane considerations obtained with reference to prisoners of war and to partially conquered nations. Now, certain nations have substituted for such humanitarianism, outrage, brutality and enforced slavery. In short, international pact and law seem to have broken down. Their restraints have yielded to the unbridled force of national greed and lust for power.

Again, in the past, the moral imperatives, independent of political treaties and laws, have exercised a wholesome constraining and restraining influence on the relations of different peoples, and have made for fraternal world-organization. Man is consti-

1 Address delivered at the Fifteenth Annual Meeting of the National Religious Education Association, New York, March 5, 1918. Republished with modifications by courtesy of *Religious Education*.

tutionally a moral being, and is, to a certain extent, governed by sentiments of justice and benevolence. These moral elements of our nature have led us to have regard for man as man, rather than for men as members of particular nations and races. Hence, in our interaction there has been a tendency to recognize and respect what we have been wont to call human rights as growing out of the essential constitution of personality. The same tendency has characterized our attitude toward men organized under political government. But alas! these fundamental moral claims are now flagrantly violated. The morally right has, with some nations, degenerated into the right of might.

Again, in the past, art has made for the unification of the race. The æsthetic consciousness is on the side of harmony. It hates chaos and loves order. It functions in the social and political spheres and tends toward unity rather than anarchy—toward peace rather than war. "Art binds together and unites the members of the nation; nay, all the members of a sphere of civilization; all those who have the same faith and the same ideals. Opinions and interests differ and produce discord; art presents in sensuous symbols the ideals which are cherished by all, and so arouses the feeling that all are, in the last analysis, of the same mind, that all recognize and adore the same ultimate and highest things."[2] When we deal with the ideal we are dealing with the universal. Thus art transcends both individualism and nationalism. It contributes toward international good will. But how ineffective it has proven along these lines during the last few tragic years. One of the first great outrages of the war was the wanton bombardment of the beautiful Rheims cathedral. The world protested against this iconoclasm, but it continued. Vandalism and robbing nations of their art treasures are features of *Kultur;* so the breach between nations widens despite the supposed unifying power of art. The nation of Bach, Beethoven, Mozart, Mendelssohn and Wagner grips with mailed fist the throat of the nation of Michelangelo,

[2] Paulsen, "A System of Ethics," trans., p. 559.

Titian, Da Vinci, Correggio and Raphael, and tries to strangle the nation of David, Delacroix and Millet. The nation of Lessing, Goethe and Schiller schools its children in a gospel of hate toward the nation of Shakespeare and Milton and a long line of glorious poets from Chaucer to Browning. The refining and organizing influences of art have given way to the brutal instincts of malevolence and greed, and a lofty idealism that bound the nations together in a golden chain of beauty finds the precious chain rudely broken. Art, like the other binding forces, has apparently failed in its work of unification.

Another force that has been operative in world-organization is religion, and especially the Christian religion. With its proclamation of the universal fatherhood of God and brotherhood of man; with the law of love as its law of social interaction; with its "Go ye into all the world and preach my gospel"—a gospel of universal membership in a kingdom of supreme values—in which every member is on a moral equality with his neighbor—the Christian religion has been promotive of a spirit of good will among men, and of harmony among the nations. But what is the case today? A nominally Christian nation joins bloody hands with a traditionally murderous nation of Mohammedan faith in wholesale assassination of one of the most ancient Christian peoples, and attempts to incite the Moslem world to warfare against nations of Christian faith, merely to enhance her own selfish interests. Furthermore, in the present crisis we find Christian nation arrayed against Christian nation; Protestant against Protestant; Catholic against Catholic; Protestant and Catholic united against Protestant and Catholic. Peoples in whose ears for centuries have rung the glad tidings of "peace on earth, good will toward men" are today gripping one another in mortal combat. The star of the East that, according to the story, guided the Wise Men to the manger of the Prince of Peace seems to have lost its radiance and directing power. Never since the star is said to have shone were men apparently farther from beating their swords into plow-shares and their spears into pruning hooks. The unifying power of him whose life illustrated even better than his parable of the Good Samaritan the highest law of human relationship is not in evidence today. Where is the power of that cross, the vision of which carried with it still another vision of a world attracted to, and unified by, the power of self-sacrificing love—"And I, if I be lifted up, will draw all men unto me"? Is the power of sacrificial love drawing the hearts of men and of nations together in the fellowship of Jesus Christ? Are not the dominant forces operating today centrifugal rather than centripetal? It is not the skeptic, or cynic, or pessimist, who asks these questions. They are the questions of thousands of earnest men and women who face the supreme crisis of human history. They bring home to us the fact that religion, even in its highest form, like international law, like morality, like art, however promotive of human brotherhood it has been, has failed in this most crucial test to prevent the dreadful work of the destructive forces of mankind. This is a fact that the sincere believer in religion must face whether he wants to or not.

In view of the failure of all of these more or less harmonizing and synthesizing forces to prevent such a gigantic war, what are we to say about world-organization after the conflict? Nations must live and sustain relations to one another. They must establish some *modus vivendi,* and it must be founded on justice. The necessity of righteousness and good will in international relations has been made more apparent than ever by this most tragic conflict. And the question arises: What organized forces are to establish such righteousness and good will among the nations? We must depend upon the very same forces that have been operative in the past; that is, upon international law, morality, art and religion, but they must be made more effective. How this may be done in the case of religion it is the aim of this paper to try to explain.

In the first place, if religion is to become powerfully effective in this direction, it must take a really ethical view of God. He must be regarded as essentially moral in his constitution; as ruling in absolute righteousness, and a being whose ultimate aim with reference to men and the world is the realization of a new heaven and a new earth wherein righteousness is to dwell. Much as believers in religion have said on this subject, the conceptions of many as expressed in belief and conduct have contradicted their words. When the nation of Martin Luther, including not merely the docile masses, but the spiritually enslaved clergy and servile university professors,[3] among whom may be numbered such religious leaders as Harnack, can accept and pray for the success of the war-program of a ruler who regards himself to be the vicegerent of the Almighty, coöperating with him in a scientifically organized movement for the triumph of the most diabolical forces the human race has ever witnessed—approving the vices of hell as though they were the virtues of heaven—this nominally Christian nation is either guilty of awful blasphemy or it has lost its vision of an ethical God. Such a conception of the Deity proves divisive rather than unifying. It recognizes merely a partisan tribal Deity who coöperates with a people to realize its own ends, however unworthy and debasing those ends may be. Its influence is promotive of national selfishness, and makes against a brotherhood of nations. Professor Leuba speaks of the utilitarian ends for which men believe in God—making him hardly more than a meat purveyor;[4] but the German conception of God is much crasser than this.[5] "*Gott mit uns*" is a God that is asked and believed to coöperate in the most damnable atrocities the human mind ever conceived in order to further low national aims.

3 On the servility of German university professors consult David Jayne Hill, *Harper's Magazine*, July, 1918, pp. 30-33.

4 *Monist*, XI, p. 571.

5 See, for example, the views of Pastors W. Lehmann ("About the German God"); H. Francke ("War Sermons"); J. Rump ("War Devotions and Memorial Services for the Fallen"); K. König ("Six War Sermons"); also Tolzien and others in "Patriotic Evangelical War Lectures."

Now, there is an important psychology here that we must reckon with. Professor Stratton, in his work on "The Psychology of the Religious Life," calls attention to the fact that religion breeds conflict, it gives birth to opposites or antitheses, and he devotes nearly the entire volume to a consideration of these conflicts. In one of his most interesting chapters[6] he points out the fact that religion is productive of both breadth and narrowness of sympathy, of both social and anti-social feelings, of both egoism and altruism. He illustrates this in pointing out the exclusiveness of some religions, such as that of the Jews, and of the catholicity of others, such as Buddhism and Christianity. He points out, also, the jealousy and intolerance of the monotheistic religions, such as Judaism, Christianity and Mohammedanism, as compared with polytheistic religions, like Buddhism. The former, like Elijah, are very jealous for their Lord, and such jealousy breeds narrowness and intolerance. It breeds exclusiveness, strife and often persecution. Now most of the conflict between narrowness and breadth of sympathy to which religion gives rise is due to wrong conceptions of the ethical nature of God. This manifests itself in many ways. God is conceived as a God of one people, rather than of others; or of one people particularly and peculiarly, and of other peoples merely generally; or a God choosing and rewarding the elect and damning the non-elect; or a God favoring only one mode of salvation peculiar to a certain people or sect, and hostile to all others; or a God of one revelation rather than of another. In short, God is a God of favoritism instead of the impartial God and father of all mankind. Such a God is not a God of justice, much less of love. Such a conception is productive of division, rather than of unity in the race. It begets strife, rather than harmony. Witness the religious wars that history records. Witness, for example, the history of the conflict between Mohammedanism and Christianity; between Protestantism and Catholicism. As a rule, religion is so involved in the life of a people

6 Pt. I, ch. II.

that it becomes an integral part of their nationalism. Historians call attention to the fact that the monotheism of the Jews was largely the outgrowth of reflection upon their own history as a people. They saw in this history a Divinity that had shaped their ends, however roughhewn they may have been. They regarded themselves a "peculiar" people, specially chosen of God. For more than a century a similar belief prevailed in America. Our wonderful history led people to believe that we are a favored nation. God's providential government reveals a partiality for America when compared with other nations. With such conceptions of a partial God, it is but a short step to making use of God for national ends, and, as illustrated in the case of the German nation today, only another step to conceiving God's willingness to coöperate in realizing ends which, in the judgment of the world, as expressed in international law, as well as in its own unwritten verdict, are regarded as unrighteous. Until the God of the race supersedes in actual belief and practice the God of nationalism; until the God and father of all mankind displaces in our belief the God of sect or of one religion rather than of another; until the God of absolute and universal righteousness takes the place in our minds and hearts of the God of partiality and favoritism, which is the God of injustice; men and nations will not be bound together in one great and glorious fraternity. The root idea of religion is the idea of God, and as is our idea of God, so will our religious life be. If it is the idea of an unrighteous Deity, our individual, national and international life will be unrighteous. A fundamental necessity in the determination of the religious basis of world-organization is an ethical conception of God.

In the second place, in our religious efforts at world-organization we must entertain and put in practice a far more ethical conception of man than we have in the past. The inalienable rights of personality must be recognized and their sancity remain inviolable. That valuation which Christianity places on man as man must be seriously reckoned with in our reconstructive efforts after the war. Or, as Kant states it, every man must be regarded as an end in himself. He must not be used merely as a means to an end. The significance of this is, that there is an essential moral equality among men. On it all political relations, whether national or international, must be based. This means, first, that within each nation a true form of government, under whatsoever name it may be known, must be democratic. "It must derive its authority and power from the consent of the governed." Autocracy is opposed to moral and political equality. It treats its subjects as tools or instruments. It builds governments of force that ignore the moral and political claims of their own people, reducing them to a docility in which they are little more than "dumb driven cattle." Thus subjugated, they are schooled from childhood in a creed of jealousy and hatred of other nations. They can be hurled in masses "into the jaws of Death" in an unrighteous war of conquest. Autocracy is upheld by militarism, and militarism means strife. On the other hand, militarism is upheld by autocracy. It first robs the people of its own nation of their rights and then proceeds to plunder other nations. It is essentially anti-social in character, and it is so because it is anti-moral. It overlooks the moral equality of men. The religion of the future must set its face like flint against this immoral view of man. It must emphasize the autonomy of the human spirit—the essential value of a soul that can determine its own conduct in the light of ideals of worth. Once it does this, democracy will assert itself in government, and autocracy, responsible for so many of the wars that have afflicted the race, will be abolished.

In the next place, this essential moral equality of men, when recognized, means that their mutual relations will become more ethically articulate, and the law of social interaction will be at least the law of justice, and in a measure the law of love,—"Thou shalt love thy neighbor as thyself,"—which being interpreted means, that just as one is under obligations to labor for the realization of the highest good in one's own person, so he is under obligations to work for the realization of the highest good in the person of others. And this highest law of human relationship must be recognized, not merely as obligatory upon individuals in their relations to other individuals, but also upon nations in their mutual relations. Morality is transcendental in its character. It overleaps the bounds of individualism. It knows not men merely, nor nations merely, nor groups of nations merely;—it knows the race. It knows man, rather than men. It is difficult for us to realize this. Just as it was hard for primitive tribes to realize any obligations to other tribes, so today, notwithstanding centuries of so-called civilization, somehow or other an international morality fails to have the binding force either of personal, community, or national morality. The righteousness that exalts a people seems largely to be a righteousness within its own borders. Egoism in a nation is just as blameworthy as egoism in an individual. In the vast group of nations, no nation liveth unto itself alone, if it is to live according to the moral law of benevolence, or according to the Christian law of love. The religion of the future must, in its practical belief, emphasize this fact far more than it has in the past. Nations are simply larger human units, and the moral law in its obligations applies just as truly to their interrelations as it does to those of individuals. Its demands are no more Utopian in the former case than in the latter. It can at least serve as an ideal or guide to conduct. As in the case of individuals, so in the case of nations, each has its rights, and in their mutual relations the moral law or the law of love requires the recognition of the rights or just claims of each. As President Wilson said in his memorable message to Congress on April 2, 1917: "We are at the beginning of an age in which it will be insisted that the same standards of conduct and of responsibility for wrong done shall be observed among nations and their governments that are observed among individuals of civilized states." And again: "It is clear that nations must in the future be governed by the same high code of honor that we demand of individuals." Of course the cynical political philosopher and "practical" stateman will regard this as "unpractical idealism." But the ethics of the Nazarene will prove far more effective in promoting a satisfactory *modus vivendi* among the nations than the revived Machiavellianism of modern Germany, or the ethics of a Nietzsche, a Treitschke, and a Bernhardi. We see the inevitable outcome of the latter in the most ghastly war of all history. There never will be peace on such a brutally egoistic basis as that laid down in the political philosophy of these writers so prized by many Germans. The doctrines of the superman with their contempt for the weak, and of war as a "biological necessity," so dear to Junkerdom, are confessedly the affirmation that "might makes right." If peace be attainable and preservable on such a basis, and the lion and the lamb are to lie down together, it will only be as the lamb lies inside of the lion. Some lamb-like pacifists and "conscientious objectors" to war may be content with such a place of residence; but physically and morally red-blooded and self-respecting men and nations not only prefer, but feel it a moral obligation to maintain the individual and national self against an unscrupulous and barbarous aggressor and destroyer. They feel so, too, in obedience to the Christian command, "Thou shalt love thy neighbor as thyself"—a command that not only includes self as the object of moral regard, but that makes it the norm according to which we are to determine our duty to others. Men and nations do feel morally responsible for their own preservation and development, and will, as a rule, defend the essential conditions of these against unjustifiable attack. Hence, as long as nations exist, war will remain a possibility. The only way to avert it is through mutual respect for fundamental rights. Both the law of benevolence and the Christian law of love demand this. Indeed, they demand more! They call for a manifestation or fuller expression of good will and fraternal regard both in feeling and in conduct.

Now, in the work of establishing a real brotherhood among

individuals and among nations, religion has the advantage over mere morality, for it can avail itself of the power of the religious sanctions in trying to realize the kingdom of righteousness. But, on the other hand, a subtle danger lurks in religion which it may be well to point out here, and which must be guarded against in our future efforts at community, national and world-organization, for it tends to subordinate the ethical element in religion, and often degenerates into an anti-social program. According to the sanest views of the psychology of religion, the whole mind as intellect, sensibility and will functions in the religious consciousness. Because of this, there is a possibility of developing a wrong sense of values in the religious life. There has been a notable tendency in human history to stress the intellectual element in religion. This has resulted in a large body of doctrine which frequently assumes extraordinary significance. The main thing, then, is to give intellectual assent to dogma and creed. Orthodoxy of belief rather than orthodoxy of life becomes the primary thing. The ethical element in religion is subordinated to intellectual belief. And how divisive and anti-social, rather than unifying, dogma has been, and how deadening to real moral endeavor! This constitutes a long and very tragic chapter in the history of Christianity, as well as of other religions.

Again, there has been another marked tendency in the history of religion and that is the substitution of the religion of feeling for the religion of will. Pietism and sentimentalism have supplanted in a large measure the ethical. Such religion is dominantly non-social, if not, indeed, anti-social in its character. It does not make for brotherhood. The pietistic monk shuts himself in a monastery and tries to work out his soul's salvation with fear and trembling, rather than to work it out by aiding his neighbor or society to work out theirs. Buddhism and Christianity have been most unfortunate victims of this substitution of solitude for solidarity. Dean Brown once said to the writer that there is a great deal of pietism that is utterly wanting in ethical quality, and that is true.

It is a kind of selfish subjectivism devoid of any real moral character. It is self-centered and non-social. It represents the minimum of true religion. Where in such pietism do we find the universality of obligation involved in the ethical law of benevolence or in the Christian law of love? Such religion does not bear the marks of a really socialized gospel. It has developed a wrong sense of values.

Again, there is in practically all religions a large element of symbolism—the religious life expressing itself in worship—in rites and ceremony. And this carries with it a dangerous tendency in evaluation. It often substitutes ritual and ceremonial for what is the real essence of religion—namely, righteousness. The great Hebrew prophets contended strongly against this misinterpretation of religion. With them it represented an erroneous estimate of the essentials of religion. Indeed, it threatened its very life—the heart of which in their conception is righteousness in God and man. Isaiah represents Jehovah as being weary of sacrifice, incense and other forms of worship—regarding them as an abomination, and calling upon the people to live a life of righteousness: "Wash you, make you clean; put away the evil of your doings from before mine eyes; cease to do evil; learn to do well; seek justice, relieve the oppressed."[7] Hosea exclaims: "I desired mercy, and not sacrifice."[8] Micah, inveighing against burnt offerings, says: "He hath shewed thee, O man, what is good, and what doth Jehovah require of thee, but to do justly, and to love mercy, and to walk humbly with thy God?"[9] And Jesus, all through the Sermon on the Mount and in the parables, in the most positive manner represents righteous living as the very core of religion.

All of these elements—the intellectual, the pietistic, the æsthetic or symbolical—have a rightful place in the religious life, but they are all subordinate, and exceedingly subordinate, to the one great dominating element, the moral. And it is because of a failure to adequately recognize and practise this element that so many sup-

[7] Isaiah 2: 10.

[8] Hosea 6: 6.

[9] Micah 6: 8.

posedly Christian nations are today in deadly conflict. All of them persist in their theological beliefs; all of them persist in pietistic communion; all of them persist in rite and ceremony; but some of them at least fail even to approximate the exemplification of the fundamental ethical requirements of their faith. Their theology, their pietism, their worship,—their religion,—have not been moralized; and unless we are willing to make, both in belief and practice, the religious basis of world-organization truly ethical, we will fail as lamentably in the future as we have in the past.

Finally, how is such a religious program to be carried forward? The answer is, by systematic religious education. Such an educational procedure involves beginning at the beginning, and that is, with the child. Here, again, we meet with a melancholy failure in the development of a true sense of values. Despite the progress that modern religious educational effort has made, there is still a widespread lack of genuine appreciation of the importance of childhood for moral and religious instruction. The premium is still placed on the adult. We have but to examine the average church program to be convinced of this. In a large number of churches we have three Sunday services—two of which are devoted to adults and one to children. In the average church the week-day services are largely services for adults. Our sermons, our hymns, our prayers, many of our week-day meetings cover chiefly the interests of grown-ups; and the lamentable condition of home religious education painfully fails to make up this deficiency in what Dr. Horace Bushnell called Christian nurture. Indeed, under a false conception of conversion, and a false apprehension of the spiritual birthright of children in most Protestant quarters, the child, as the late Professor George P. Fisher once remarked to the writer, is regarded as an alien to the Commonwealth of Israel. Instead of being born into the church and treated as a member of the household of faith, he must serve his probation as a heathen, and await the dawn of adolescence when he will have developed sufficient maturity of mind to interpret and give intellectual assent to a creed. The absurdity and tragedy of it all are manifest when we take into consideration the ethical character of religion, and the fact that childhood is preëminently the period for establishing the individual in habits of virtue. There may be some exaggeration in Dr. G. Stanley Hall's affirmation, that the moral and spiritual destiny of the average person is determined in the first ten years of his life; but, to anyone who has studied the psychology of moral and spiritual development, it is evident that Hall is dealing with far more than a half-truth. The receptivity and plasticity of the child make it possible for those to whom his most vital interests are committed to really save him or damn him. And, as we establish children in right thinking and right living, so we establish the community, the state, the nation, and ultimately the nations in their reciprocal relations. In more ways than one is Wordsworth's statement true, "The child is father to the man." It is preëminently true in the moral and religious sphere. The Kingdom of God and his righteousness will never make the progress on earth that they should make until the scales really fall from our eyes, and we gain a true vision of our duty to the child in establishing him in personal and community righteousness, and thus pave the way for the application of the law of righteousness in the state and among the nations of the earth.

In still another way, to one who is convinced of the supremacy of moral and spiritual worths and of the ethical aim of all true religion, is the lamentable failure to develop a true sense of values manifest. Professor Pratt calls attention in his "Psychology of Religious Belief" to what he regards to be a fact, that in the average American community, "we find our friends and neighbors, of all degrees of education and intellectual ability, almost to a man accepting God as one of the best recognized realities of their world and as simply not to be questioned."[10] That statement is in the main true. In other words, we are a religious people. And

[10] Page 231.

yet, notwithstanding this fact, so far as thoroughgoing, systematic religious education is concerned, when compared with the time and efforts devoted to education along other lines, and its quality, it suffers painfully. In nearly all of the states, five days a week, of at least four or five hours each, are given to what we call secular education, as against one day per week, of one hour each, to religious instruction and worship. In secular education we have, on the whole, a trained body of teachers. In religious education we are dependent largely on amateurs. In most places religion is not allowed a voice in our schools, so far as *systematic* training is concerned, and in comparatively few communities has a systematic course of moral training even been introduced. What does all this mean? Does it not mean that we err tremendously in our sense of values? If there is any doubt concerning this, reflect for a moment on the possibility of organizing a community on a basis of the vices instead of the virtues. Try to found a community on sensuality, falsehood, dishonesty, injustice, hate and murder, and see how far you will succeed. Society could not exist on such a basis. Were the German people to put into practice among themselves the vices and crimes they have committed against other peoples, their existence as a nation would be exceedingly short-lived. The vices are anti-social in their character. The virtues are social: they make for unity, for organization. And what is true of communities is true of states and nations—not only in their internal relations but in their relations to other nations. The virtues make for national and international organization. Now, religion deals with these sovereign values, and yet, comparatively speaking, we—a religious people—relegate them to the background in our educational schemes. We will never succeed in world-organization until we genuinely appreciate the unifying power of the virtues, the harmonizing and binding force of righteousness, and systematically train a generation from childhood in a knowledge and an appreciation of their supreme worth, and try to mould their wills in conformity to their requirements.

But, as Herbert Spencer wisely remarks, we have not an ideal environment in which to work out our ideals. And that is eminently true in this case; therefore, wisdom dictates that we try to do our work with reference to the conditions of the actual environment in which we are placed. If, for apparently good reasons, it be not expedient under present conditions to introduce systematic religious education into the public schools, it is possible for us to make provision in some other way for religion to have its rightful place in the general training of our children. This would require a religious school organization, with a curriculum that interprets religion as ethical in its aim. It would require a scientifically graded moral scheme with its corresponding religious sanctions; also the creation of a literature to meet these demands. It would require, at least, three sessions a week. It should be separate from the Sunday school, where, with present conditions, sectarianism still enters into education, and yet it should be supplementary to it. It would call for a specially trained teaching force; and for skilled professional supervision. All this ought to be done; it can be done; and it must be done. We must do it in the interests of the individual, of the family, of the community, of the state, of the nation, and of the brotherhood of nations. It is a thoroughly practicable scheme. The literature exists already; colleges, schools of religion, and theological seminaries can easily become training schools for the preparation of religious teachers. The only difficulty in the way, which is, indeed, a serious one, but by no means insuperable, is the time-schedule of the children. In my own judgment, if a real effort were made by the churches of any community, a plan could be formulated in relation to the public schools whereby the children would become available for such religious instruction. If the community is a religious one, it has a right to, and must insist upon, having the children a fair share of the time for such purposes. If the moral and spiritual values are the supreme values of society, then it is in the interests of society itself that these values should receive proper recognition in formal education for citizenship. The real trouble is, that the churches are not really in earnest concerning this important matter. It has taken an awful social cataclysm to make us realize that nations, like families and communities, can hang together on no other basis than the cardinal virtues, and that something more than a mere formal recognition of these virtues is required for world-organization. Men and nations must be disciplined in them, and the way to do this is to begin in childhood. If the schooling of a nation in a gospel of national egoism and hate be largely responsible for the present war, with the brutal indifference of the German people to moral considerations in provoking it and to humane methods of waging it, why is it not possible to school the nations in those things that make for good will and world-organization? To doubt it is to doubt the might of right.

In conclusion, my plea is, that, in our efforts at world re-organization, so far as religion is concerned, we adequately reckon with its ethical character. Let us take, first, an ethical view of God—that he is a righteous being, that he deals justly with all men and all nations, that he cannot be used by any individual or nation for unrighteous ends, that he is the father of us all, and that he coöperates with men in their efforts to bring in the reign of righteousness upon earth. And, secondly, let us take a more ethical view of man; recognizing the worth and inalienable rights of personality; that no man may be used merely as a means, but must be regarded as an end in himself; and thus, whatever may be the outward form of government, it must in essence be democratic, rather than autocratic; that the law of interaction among nations must be the same as the law among individuals—the law of benevolence or the law of love. Let us develop a true sense of values in religion that will place emphasis on the voluntaristic or ethical element rather than on either the intellectual, pietistic and symbolical or æsthetic. Finally, let us try to realize this program by thorough, systematic religious education in which we shall emphasize the interests of the child rather than the interests of the adult; by giving an ethical interpretation to the curriculum; by organizing a trained body of teachers; and by insisting that a fair amount of the child's time and effort shall be devoted to education in the supreme values of society. If we act on this program, if we make this really the religious basis of world re-organization, we will make long strides toward the dawn of a better day, when nations shall seek war no more; and the kingdoms of this world shall become the kingdoms of our righteous God and his Christ, whose gospel and life teach the universal fatherhood of God and the universal brotherhood of man.